ENJOYING MORE
POETRY

Sadler & Hayllar

M

Copyright © R. K. Sadler and T. A. S. Hayllar 1983

First published 1983 by
THE MACMILLAN COMPANY OF AUSTRALIA PTY LTD
107 Moray Street, South Melbourne 3205
6 Clarke Street, Crows Nest 2065
Reprinted 1984, 1985, 1986, 1987, 1988, 1989, 1990

Associated companies and representatives
throughout the world

National Library of Australia
cataloguing in publication data
Sadler, R. K. (Rex Kevin).
    Enjoying more poetry.

    For secondary school students.
    Includes index.
    ISBN 0 333 35655 1.

    1. English poetry. I. Hayllar, T. A. S.
    (Thomas Albert S.). II. Title.

821'.008

Set in Century by Savage & Co. Pty Ltd, Brisbane
Printed in Hong Kong

Contents

7. Personification   70

8. The World of Animals   75

9. Writing Your Own Poems   88

14. Story-Poems   **135**

15. Rhythm   **147**

16. Poems That Mock   **155**

17. Shapely Poems   **164**

18. Pairs of Poems   **170**

Preface

A poem is not a delicate piece of pottery that
clumsy hands may drop and break in pieces. It
can be analysed, dissected, put under the
microscope; and the closer and more detailed
the examination, the more one finds to admire,
as with any work of art.

from *Feet on the Ground*
by Margaret J. O'Donnell

Poetry, like other fine arts, exists to be enjoyed and appreciated. The difficult task facing any teacher is that of developing this sense of appreciation and enjoyment in students who initially 'don't like poetry'.

Obviously, to some extent appreciation grows out of understanding. Students must learn to examine poems critically and thoughtfully, to see what the poet is driving at, to consider how well he or she is saying it, and so on. This does require work of some sort, but there is no other way to develop appreciation of poetry. The work can be at the talking level, with teachers and students discussing aspects of a poem and trying to refine their awareness of its impact on them by thoughtful analysis. It can also be at the writing level, with students attentively evaluating and communicating, in written form, the achievement and effect of a poem.

A sensitive teaching approach is needed — one that combines discussion and writing, one that examines ideas and feelings, one that encourages appreciation of the poetry of others while also giving room for the student to try his or her own hand at creating poetry — an approach that above all is built upon teacher-enthusiasm for poetry.

As its title suggests, this book adopts an approach similar to that of *Enjoying Poetry*. We have tried to offer raw material which we believe can be shaped into a poetry course aimed at developing an appreciation and an enjoyment of poetry. In particular, we have tried to present material that carries a high level of interest for students, while not neglecting the needs of quality. Furthermore, special units throughout the book provide a way of introducing students to the basics of poetry technique. In short, we believe that teachers will find this to be a poetry book that students can learn from and enjoy.

With poetry, as with many other pursuits in life, understanding brings enjoyment.

1. The Five Senses

Poets want to share their feelings and experiences with us, and they try to make them as vivid as possible. In order to develop this keener awareness, poets delight whenever they can in engaging our five senses — sight, sound, smell, touch and taste.

As you read through each of the following poems, let the poet's imagination and power over words take control of your senses.

Sight

Even though this beautiful description of a stallion was written more than a hundred years ago, the poet's word-painting is so effective that we can imagine the magnificent creature standing beside us now.

A GIGANTIC BEAUTY OF A STALLION

A gigantic beauty of a stallion, fresh and responsive to my caresses.
Head high in the forehead, wide between the ears,
Limbs glossy and supple, tail dusting the ground,
Eyes full of sparkling wickedness, ears finely cut, flexibly moving.
His nostrils dilate as my heels embrace him,
His well-built limbs tremble with pleasure as we race around and
    return.

WALT WHITMAN

Far too often we take for granted the beautiful things around us. The poet enables us to look with clearer vision at the beauty to be found in nature.

SWIFT THINGS ARE BEAUTIFUL

Swift things are beautiful:
Swallows and deer,
And lightning that falls
Bright-veined and clear,
Rivers and meteors,
Wind in the wheat,
The strong-withered horse,
The runner's sure feet.

And slow things are beautiful:
The closing of day,
The pause of the wave
That curves downward to spray,
The ember that crumbles,
The opening flower,
And the ox that moves on
In the quiet of power.

ELIZABETH COATSWORTH

Sound

Just as sights are important to the poet, so too are sounds. Poets are extremely conscious of the need to arrange sounds skilfully within their poems to evoke particular moods, feelings and actions. They are also very sensitive to the sounds around them, as the following poem reveals.

PLEASANT SOUNDS

The rustling of leaves under the feet in woods and under hedges;
The crumpling of cat-ice and snow down wood-rides, narrow
  lanes and every street causeway;
Rustling through a wood or rather rushing, while the wind halloos
  in the oak top like thunder;
The rustle of birds' wings startled from their nests or
  flying unseen into the bushes;
The whizzing of larger birds overhead in a wood, such as
  crows, puddocks, buzzards;
The trample of robins and woodlarks on the brown leaves,
  and the patter of squirrels on the green moss;
The fall of an acorn on the ground, the pattering of nuts
  on the hazel branches as they fall from ripeness;
The flirt of the groundlark's wing from the stubbles — how sweet
  such pictures on dewy mornings, when the dew flashes
  from its brown feathers!

JOHN CLARE

Sounds Pleasant and Unpleasant

Now write down some pleasant and unpleasant sounds of your own. The
first ones have been done to start you off.

	Pleasant	Unpleasant
(1)	The cheeping of chicks	The shriek of chalk on a blackboard
(2)		
(3)		
(4)		
(5)		
(6)		

Smell

Of the five senses, poets have been least concerned with the sense of smell. To make up for this, the poet Christopher Morley is delighted to present us with a poem full of smells. Edward Thomas is another poet who delights in smells — those that come from his garden. Are your noses alert?

SMELLS

Why is it that the poets tell
So little of the sense of smell?
These are the odours I love well:

The smell of coffee freshly ground;
Or rich plum pudding, holly crowned;
Or onions fried and deeply browned.

The fragrance of a fumy pipe;
The smell of apples, newly ripe;
And printers' ink on leaden type.

Woods by moonlight in September
Breathe most sweet; and I remember
Many a smoky camp-fire ember.

Camphor, turpentine, and tea,
The balsam of a Christmas tree,
These are whiffs of gramarye ...
A ship smells best of all to me!

CHRISTOPHER MORLEY

DIGGING

Today I think
Only with scents, — scents dead leaves yield,
And bracken, and wild carrot's seed,
And the square mustard field;

Odours that rise
When the spade wounds the root of tree,
Rose, currant, raspberry, or goutweed,
Rhubarb or celery;

The smoke's smell, too,
Flowing from where a bonfire burns
The dead, the waste, the dangerous,
And all to sweetness turns.

It is enough
To smell, to crumble the dark earth,
While the robin sings over again
Sad songs of Autumn mirth.

EDWARD THOMAS

The poet J. Charles has created a very pleasing poem by joining together the senses of smell and hearing.

SOUNDS AND SMELLS

So many sounds bring delight;
The crunch of shoes on a frosty night,
The pouring of tea, the wind in the trees,
The swishing of cornfields in the breeze.

The joy of smells, too, will never pass;
I love the scent of new-mown grass,
The salty tang of a sandy beach,
And the gentle fragrance of a peach.

J. CHARLES

For You to Do

(1) Most shops have smells of their own. Write down the names of some shops and the kinds of smells you associate with them.
(2) What places (or people) do you associate with the following smells?

(a) fresh coffee	(e) chlorine	(i) seaweed
(b) antiseptic	(f) petrol	(j) steak
(c) tar	(g) incense	(k) hot bread
(d) perfume	(h) fresh paint	(l) cigarette smoke

Touch

John Thompson's poem 'The Sunbather' captures the feelings we've all experienced lying in the sun on the beach. John Walsh's poem 'First Dip' then presents us with the sensations that come upon us when we first enter the water.

THE SUNBATHER

I shield my face. My eyes are closed. I spin
With nearing sleep. I am dissolved within
Myself, and softened like a ripening fruit.
I swing in a red-hazy void, I sway
With tides of blind heat. From a far-off sphere,
Like scratchings on a pillow, voices I hear
And thundering waves and thuds of passing feet;
For there, out there beyond me, lads and girls
In dazzling colours and with gleaming skin
Through sands of gold and surfs of opal run;

They dive beneath the long green claw which curls
Above them; on the white comber they shoot
Shoreward; many in a slow spiral melt
Like me into oblivion under the sun.

JOHN THOMPSON

FIRST DIP

Wave after wavelet goes
Coldly over your toes
And sinks down into the stones.
Another mounts to your knees,
Icy, as if to freeze
Flesh and marrow and bones.
And now another, a higher,
Yellow with foam, and dire
With weed from yesterday's storm.
With a gasp you greet it —
Your shoulders stoop to meet it —
And you find ... you find ...
    Ah-h-h-h!
You find that the water's warm!

JOHN WALSH

Most people dislike touching slimy things, but here's one poet that doesn't mind at all.

SLIMY THINGS

I can touch anything that is something
But best of all I love touching slimy things,
Like seaweed that you slip on
And mud that squeezes up between your toes.
Dark ooey slippery mud.
It's murky and slurpy
And moves right up my spine.
I love sinking down into it
I love to rub it right up my legs.
I'd love to have a mud swimming pool
And to plunge into it
And to slurp around
Up and down, around and around and around.

GEORGINA GOSS

A Sense of Touch

Next to each of the adjectives in the column, write down as many appropriate words and phrases as you can. A couple of examples have been given to start you off. (The exercise continues overleaf.)

Cold	a dog's nose, water pipes in winter
Hot	
Wet	
Sticky	
Soft	
Hard	
Prickly	
Slimy	

Furry	
Smooth	
Rough	
Curved	

Taste

Have you ever tried to describe what something tastes like? Sometimes this can be quite difficult. In 'Poems', Anne Holman describes the effect on her when she eats apples, honeycomb and ice cream.

POEMS

The apples
this year
are crisp.
When I bite
them they
bite back.
I like
the way
the juice
runs down
my chin.

My tooth
shrieks
to honeycomb
and
I answer
with
a whip
from
my spine.

And
ice cream
spears
my brain
to stars
behind
my eyes.

ANNE HOLMAN

In the poem below, the poet is apologizing for eating some plums. But he is also telling us something else. What is it?

THIS IS JUST TO SAY

I have eaten
the plums
that were in
the icebox

and which
you were probably
saving
for breakfast

Forgive me
they were delicious
so sweet
and so cold

WILLIAM CARLOS WILLIAMS

Likes

Complete the table by filling in some of the things you like to eat and drink.

THINGS I LIKE TO EAT	THINGS I LIKE TO DRINK

2. In the Outback

Written some fifty years ago, this poem portrays a woman's feelings about life in the Australian outback. Life was never easy. Not only did the shearer's wife have to work hard doing farming and household chores; she also had another very difficult problem to face — that of loneliness.

THE SHEARER'S WIFE

Before the glare o' dawn I rise
To milk the sleepy cows, an' shake
The droving dust from tired eyes,
Look round the rabbit traps, then bake
    The children's bread.
There's hay to stook, an' beans to hoe,
An' ferns to cut in the scrub below.
Women must work, when men must go
    Shearing from shed to shed.

I patch an' darn, now evening comes,
An' tired I am with labour sore,
Tired o' the bush, the cows, the gums,
Tired, but must dree for long months more
    What no tongue tells.
The moon is lonely in the sky,
Lonely the bush, an' lonely I
Stare down the track no horse draws nigh
    An' start ... at the cattle bells.

LOUIS ESSON

The Shearer's Wife — Reading for meaning
(1) Why are the cows sleepy?
(2) Men '... must go / Shearing from shed to shed'. What picture do these words give you?

(3) How do you know that the shearer's wife works very hard?

(4) Why does the shearer's wife have to work so hard?

(5) What are her feelings about country life?

(6) The word 'dree' means 'suffer'. In what way does the wife suffer?

(7) Why do you think life is so lonely for the shearer's wife?

(8) What are your feelings towards this woman? Why?

(9) What is the meaning of 'the track no horse draws nigh'?

(10) 'The Shearer's Wife' was written many years ago. Do you think the events described in the poem could take place today? Why or why not?

Bill Harney, former Warden of Ayers Rock in Central Australia, was a famous Australian bushman who wrote many books about the outback. He explains in graphic detail how he came to write the poem 'West of Alice'.

Poet's Corner

In about 1953 I was offsiding to Sam Irvine on a grader, doing some levelling along the road to Alice Springs. As we were travelling along through some high hills the 100 horsepower cat. was roaring and kicking up a great noise and the animals and birds were clearing out as hard as they could, but some [Aboriginal] kiddies came out and ran alongside us. The grader with its great shining blade kept knocking the trees aside and pushing the flowers away and rolling back the earth so that the blood-red ground showed underneath. And all the time a great cut kept stretching out behind us where I could remember there were once only camel pads.

All of a sudden a poem began to scratch round in my head. Like they always do, a few lines kept coming to me, and then a few more, and then a few more, till the whole poem was complete. I memorized it then, and kept saying it over to myself — perhaps while the cat. was grinding along or perhaps while I was lying in my bed under those great blazing stars up there — and every now and then I'd correct a word that seemed wrong to me. When the whole thing was complete I recited it at a bit of a party one night when we were camped at Kulgera, 170 miles [274 km] south-west of Alice Springs. I'll never forget that night I first recited 'West of Alice'. There was twenty degrees of frost and my bed outside the caravan was as white as if it had a sheet over it.

Bill Harney

WEST OF ALICE

We are travelling west of Alice Springs, and Sam is at the wheel;
Riding the diesel-grader I am watching its blade of steel
Roll back the dark-red sandy loam or grind the limestones grey,
And the wheels whirl in a red-dust swirl along the new highway.

We pass where Sturt-peas clothe the earth with a scarlet sweep of
   flowers,
And burst through green acacia-trees that send down golden
   showers;
The parakeelia's purple blooms are crushed in the dry, red sand
When the bright blade sweeps as the grader creeps over the stern,
   strange land.

The mulga, mallee, desert-oaks fall prostrate as we pass,
The lizards, pigeons, porcupines crouch low in stone and grass;
We brush the spinifex aside; tear down the bush-rat's shade,
And the desert mole in its sandhill hole digs faster from our blade.

The honey-ants are rooted out to roll upon the sand,
But ever the ramping, stamping fiend goes roaring through the land;
The tyres grind and the steel blade cuts the pads where camels trod
And claws at the ground of a stony mound where tribesmen praised
   their God.

We cross the desert rivers, formed when the world was new,
And churn to dust the fossil-bones of the giant kangaroo;
I wave to naked native kids upon Erldunda's plain,
And we fill our tank where the black men drank from rock-holes filled
   by rain.

We camp in Kulgera's weathered hills, scarred core of an ancient
    range,
Where the camp-fire flame throws out its light on a scene that is ever
    strange
As a dingo wails by the painted wall of a sacred cave near by
And the stars shine bright as we lie at night beneath a frosty sky.

We rise as mulga-parakeets go whirling through the dawn,
We see old star-man Manbuk rise from depths of midnight drawn;
We hear the grader's engine roar with Sam behind the wheel,
And I sing my song as we plunge along to the chatter of wheel and
    steel.

W. E. ('BILL') HARNEY

West of Alice — Looking closely

(1)   What words in the poem tell you that the countryside is full of
      beauty?
(2)   How do the animals react to the appearance of the grader?
(3)   Do you think the poet enjoyed his work? Give your reasons.
(4)   What evidence can you find to suggest that the Aborigines had
      inhabited this land for a very long time?
(5)   Levelling the road could be called 'progress'. What are your feelings
      about the grader?
(6)   'But ever the ramping, stamping fiend goes roaring through the
      land . . . .' What is Bill Harney's attitude to the grader?

Here is a poem about sale-time in the outback. It's full of dust and heat, soiled clothes and bellowing cattle. Children, of course, love sale-time.

SALE-TIME

There's dust and loud cracking of whips
On the hot dry plain:
The stockmen are droving the cattle in
To the sales again.

The children will hurry from school,
When their lessons are done,
To clamber about on the stockyard rails
In the glaring sun.

There'll be bidding and buying today;
There'll be hustling and oaths;
And children they worship the strong brown men
In the coarse soiled clothes.

They love to be watching the sight
Of the auctioning
Of bullocks and heifers and calves, and hear
All the bellowing.

They'll be dreaming all during the week
When the sales are over,
Though teacher be speaking of spelling and sums,
Of the bullock-drover.

REX INGAMELLS

You will understand this poem better if you are aware of the difference between a squatter and a selector. To put it simply, the *squatter* went out into the unsettled countryside and, when he found a good place, set up his farm. He did not buy the land he 'squatted' on. Later on, the *selector* was allowed by the government to purchase land he had 'selected' from the squatter's property. Naturally, when this happened the squatter would often become antagonistic towards the selector and a feud would begin.

THE FIRE AT ROSS'S FARM

The squatter saw his pastures wide
    Decrease, as one by one
The farmers moving to the west
    Selected on his run;
Selectors took the water up
    And all the black-soil round;
The best grass-land the squatter had
    Was spoilt by Ross's ground.

Now many schemes to shift old Ross
    Had racked the squatter's brains,
But Sandy had the stubborn blood
    Of Scotland in his veins;
He held the land and fenced it in,
    He cleared and ploughed the soil,
And year by year a richer crop
    Repaid him for his toil.

Between the homes for many years
    The devil left his tracks:
The squatter 'pounded Ross's stock,
    And Sandy 'pounded Black's.
A well upon the lower run
    Was filled with earth and logs,
And Black laid baits about the farm
    To poison Ross's dogs.

It was, indeed, a deadly feud
  Of class and creed and race,
So Fate supplied a Romeo
  And a Juliet in the case;
And more than once across the flats,
  Beneath the Southern Cross,
Young Robert Black was seen to ride
  With pretty Jenny Ross.

One Christmas time, when months of drought
  Had parched the western creeks,
The bush-fires started in the north
  And travelled south for weeks.
At night along the river-side
  The scene was grand and strange —
The hill-fires looked like lighted streets
  Of cities in the range.

The cattle-tracks between the trees
  Were like long dusky aisles,
And on a sudden breeze the fire
  Would sweep along for miles;
Like sounds of distant musketry
  It crackled through the brakes,
And o'er the flat of silver grass
  It hissed like angry snakes.

It leapt across the flowing streams
  And raced the pastures through;
It climbed the trees, and lit the boughs,
  And fierce and fiercer grew.
The bees fell stifled in the smoke
  Or perished in their hives,
And with the stock the kangaroos
  Went flying for their lives.

The sun had set on Christmas Eve,
  When through the scrub-lands wide
Young Robert Black came riding home
  As only natives ride.
He galloped to the homestead door
  And gave the first alarm:
'The fire is past the granite spur,
  And close to Ross's farm.

'Now, father, send the men at once,
  They don't be wanted here;
Poor Ross's wheat is all he has
  To pull him through the year.'
'Then let it burn,' the squatter said;
  'I'd like to see it done —
I'd bless the fire if it would clear
  Selectors from the run.

'Go if you will,' the squatter said,
  'You shall not take the men —
Go out and join your precious friends,
  But don't come here again.'
'I won't come back,' young Robert cried,
  And, reckless in his ire,
He sharply turned the horse's head
  And galloped towards the fire.

And there for three long weary hours,
  Half-blind with smoke and heat,
Old Ross and Robert fought the flames
  That neared the ripened wheat.
The farmer's hand was nerved by fear
  Of danger and of loss;
And Robert fought the stubborn foe
  For love of Jenny Ross.

But serpent-like the curves and lines
  Slipped past them, and between,
Until they reached the boundary where
  The old coach-road had been.
'The track is now our only hope,
  There we must stand,' cried Ross,
'For naught on earth can stop the fire
  If once it gets across.'

Then came a cruel gust of wind,
  And, with a fiendish rush,
The flames leapt o'er the narrow path
  And lit the fence of brush.
'The crop must burn!' the farmer cried,
  'We cannot save it now,'
And down upon the blackened ground
  He dashed his ragged bough.

But wildly, in a rush of hope,
　His heart began to beat,
For o'er the crackling fire he heard
　The sound of horses' feet.
'Here's help at last,' young Robert cried,
　And even as he spoke
The squatter with a dozen men
　Came racing through the smoke.

Down on the ground the stockmen jumped
　And bared each brawny arm;
They tore green branches from the trees
　And fought for Ross's farm;
And when before the gallant band
　The beaten flames gave way,
Two grimy hands in friendship joined —
　And it was Christmas Day.

HENRY LAWSON

The Fire at Ross's Farm — Thinking about it

(1)　Why did the squatter dislike Ross?

(2)　What did Ross's and Black's hatred for each other lead them to do?

(3)　Why did the poet refer to Robert Black and Jenny Ross as 'a Romeo and a Juliet'?

(4)　What did the bushfire look like at night?

(5)　On a sudden breeze, what kind of sounds did the bushfire make?

(6)　How do you know that the bushfire could jump across obstacles?

(7)　What would have happened to Ross if his wheat crop had not been saved?

(8)　How did Black first respond to his son's request for help?

(9)　What did Robert Black then do?

(10)　Why was Ross about to give up trying to put out the fire?

(11)　What method did the firefighters use to put out the fire?

(12)　What words in the last stanza suggest that there would be no more hatred between Ross and Black?

The hare is a very timid creature. Can you imagine a hare so utterly exhausted by the sun's heat that it is unwilling, even at the approach of a human, to leave its little strip of shade?

HARE IN SUMMER

In the little strip of shade
that a strainer-post has made,
squats a weakly panting hare.
All day he has squatted there.
Only with the shade he shifts.
As I approach, he slowly lifts
his goggling eyes, but will not run,
fearing me less than the naked sun.

FLEXMORE HUDSON

Poet's Corner

I spent three years (1939–1941) in the north of South Australia — in the little township of Hammond, about 20 miles [32 km] from Quorn and the Flinders Ranges.

On top of a grasshopper plague there came a drought that lasted two years. The vast plain drifted badly; even kurrajongs perished; some farmers kept their cows alive by feeding them branches cut down from pepper trees and umbrella trees. Dust storms raged night and day; even in the calms, willy-willies, tall as Mt Remarkable, suddenly appeared and rushed crazily miles and miles across the plain. And the wedge-tail eagles came down from the Ranges to hunt.

The school children used to tell me how they had run down hares in the mid-day heat, but I thought they were drawing the long bow, till one day, not far from the township, I came upon a hare cowering in the shade of a strainer-post. It was 117 degrees [47°C] in the shade; heat and thirst had made him groggy. He slued his eyes round at my approach, made a feeble move into the sun, and then shrank back into the thin shade. I could easily have caught him.

I remember that the day on which I wrote the poem was hot. On such days one feels a poem should be short.

Flexmore Hudson

The drought just described by Flexmore Hudson is probably the same one
that forms the subject of our next poem, also by Hudson.

DROUGHT

Midsummer noon; and the timbered walls
start in the heat,
and the children sag listlessly over the desks
with bloodless faces oozing sweat
sipped by the stinging flies.
Outside, the tall sun fades the shabby mallee,
and drives the ants deep underground;
the stony drift-sand shrivels
the drab sparse plants:
there's not a cloud in all the sky to cast
a shadow on the tremulous plain.
Stirless the windmills; thirsty cattle, standing
despondently about the empty tanks,
stamping and tossing their heads,
in torment of the flies from dawn to dark.
For ten parched days it has been like this
and, although I love the desert, I
have found myself,
              dreaming
of upright gums by a mountain creek
where the red boronia blooms,
where the bell-birds chime through the morning mists,
and greenness can hide from the sun;
of rock-holes where the brumbies slink
like swift cloud-shadows from the gidgee-scrub
to drink when the moon is low.
And as I stoop to drink, I too,
just as I raise my cupped hands to my lips,
I am recalled to this drought-stricken plain
by the petulant question
of a summer-wearied child.

FLEXMORE HUDSON

Drought — Closer scrutiny

(1) It is extremely hot in the classroom. What words of the poet
emphasize this?

(2) How do the ants react to the heat?

(3) How does the first half of the poem (the first 15 lines) differ from the second?

(4) How do you know that there is no wind or water?

(5) Notice how the word 'dreaming' has a line of its own. Why do you think the poet has done this? What does the poet dream about?

(6) What brings the poet back from his dreaming to the harsh reality of the stifling classroom?

(7) What does he mean by the phrase 'summer-wearied child'?

(8) In 'Drought', what important experience has the poet tried to re-create so that he can share it with you, his reader?

TANGMALANGALOO

The bishop sat in lordly state and purple cap sublime,
And galvanized the old bush church at Confirmation time;
And all the kids were mustered up from fifty miles around,
With Sunday clothes, and staring eyes, and ignorance profound.
Now was it fate, or was it grace, whereby they yarded too
An overgrown two-storey lad from Tangmalangaloo?

A hefty son of virgin soil, where nature has her fling,
And grows the trefoil three feet high and mats it in the spring;
Where mighty hills uplift their heads to pierce the welkin's rim,
And trees sprout up a hundred feet before they shoot a limb;
There everything is big and grand, and men are giants too —
But Christian Knowledge wilts, alas, at Tangmalangaloo.

The bishop summed the youngsters up, as bishops only can;
He cast a searching glance around, then fixed upon his man.
But glum and dumb and undismayed through every bout he sat;
He seemed to think that he was there, but wasn't sure of that.
The bishop gave a scornful look, as bishops sometimes do,
And glared right through the pagan in from Tangmalangaloo.

'Come tell me, boy,' his lordship said in crushing tones severe,
'Come tell me why is Christmas Day the greatest of the year?
How is it that around the world we celebrate that day
And send a name upon a card to those who're far away?
Why is it wandering ones return with smiles and greetings, too?'
A squall of knowledge hit the lad from Tangmalangaloo.

He gave a lurch which set a-shake the vases on the shelf,
He knocked the benches all askew, up-ending of himself.
And oh, how pleased his lordship was, and how he smiled to say,
'That's good, my boy. Come, tell me now; and what is Christmas
   Day?'
The ready answer bared a fact no bishop ever knew —
'It's the day before the races out at Tangmalangaloo.'

JOHN O'BRIEN

Tangmalangaloo — Your response

(1)   What did you notice about the bishop's appearance?
(2)   What did the church people do when they knew that the bishop would
      be present at the bush church?
(3)   How did the children react to the appearance of the bishop?
(4)   What do the words 'two-storey' tell you about the lad from Tang-
      malangaloo?
(5)   What kind of place was Tangmalangaloo?
(6)   How did the lad from Tangmalangaloo act during the bishop's talk?
(7)   Why do you think the lad from Tangmalangaloo 'knocked the
      benches all askew'?
(8)   What was surprising about the boy's answer?
(9)   Which word best describes this poem: 'serious', 'humorous', 'sorrow-
      ful', or 'monotonous'?
(10) What comments would you make about the personality of the lad
      from Tangmalangaloo?

The poet Kenneth Slessor gives us an impression of country towns which
is very different from our present-day picture of them. He is writing about
the sleepy little country towns of the years before the arrival in force of
the motorcar.

COUNTRY TOWNS

Country towns, with your willows and squares,
And farmers bouncing on barrel mares
To public-houses of yellow wood
With '1860' over their doors,
And that mysterious race of Hogans
Which always keeps General Stores. . . .

At the School of Arts, a broadsheet lies
Sprayed with the sarcasm of flies:
'The Great Golightly Family
Of Entertainers Here To-night'—
Dated a year and a half ago,
But left there, less from carelessness
Than from a wish to seem polite.

Verandas baked with musky sleep,
Mulberry faces dozing deep,
And dogs that lick the sunlight up
Like paste of gold — or, roused in vain
By far, mysterious buggy-wheels,
Lower their ears, and drowse again. . . .

Country towns with your schooner bees,
And locusts burnt in the pepper-trees,
Drown me with syrups, arch your boughs,
Find me a bench, and let me snore,
Till, charged with ale and unconcern,
I'll think it's noon at half-past four!

KENNETH SLESSOR

Kenneth Slessor's comments about the poem are interesting: 'The town of "Country Towns" is not meant to be any town in particular. It is simply a general picture of Australian country towns as I have known them. I did see, printed on a brown and peeling poster, the news that "The Great Golightly Family of Entertainers" had been there in the past. As I remember it, their principal entertainment was playing the musical glasses.'

Perhaps some of you are wondering what the School of Arts was? There are Schools of Arts still in existence today. These buildings were used for dances, concerts and meetings. If you come across one, you will probably find that it has a library as well.

The expression 'schooner bees' has often puzzled readers. Douglas Stewart, himself a poet and a personal friend of Kenneth Slessor, records the response he received from the poet about these bees: ' "Schooner bees", incidentally, I learnt from the master's own lips, are simply large bees that look like sailing ships; bumble bees, I suppose.'

'The Cattle-dog's Death' is a very moving poem. Such is their love for their dying dog that the parched stockmen give it the last of their water.

THE CATTLE-DOG'S DEATH

The plains lay bare on the homeward route,
And the march was heavy on man and brute;
For the Spirit of Drouth was on all the land,
And the white heat danced on the glowing sand.

The best of our cattle-dogs lagged at last;
His strength gave out ere the plains were passed;
And our hearts were sad as he crept and laid
His languid limbs in the nearest shade.

He saved our lives in the years gone by,
When no one dreamed of the danger nigh,
And treacherous blacks in the darkness crept
On the silent camp where the white men slept.

'Rover is dying,' a stockman said,
As he knelt and lifted the shaggy head;
' 'Tis a long day's march ere the run be near,
And he's going fast; shall we leave him here?'

But the super cried, 'There's an answer there!'
As he raised a tuft of the dog's grey hair;
And, strangely vivid, each man descried
The old spear-mark on the shaggy hide.

We laid a bluey and coat across
A camp-pack strapped on the lightest horse,
Then raised the dog to his deathbed high,
And brought him far 'neath the burning sky.

At the kindly touch of the stockmen rude
His eyes grew human with gratitude;
And though we were parched, when his eyes grew dim
The last of our water was given to him.

The super's daughter we knew would chide
If we left the dog in the desert wide;
So we carried him home o'er the burning sand
For a parting stroke from her small white hand.

But long ere the station was seen ahead,
His pain was o'er, for Rover was dead;
And the folks all knew by our looks of gloom
'Twas a comrade's corpse that we carried home.

HENRY LAWSON

The Cattle-dog's Death — Understanding the poem

(1) What words of the poet give the feeling of intense heat?
(2) What was the first indication that Rover was dying?
(3) In the past, how had Rover saved the men's lives?
(4) What impression do you have of Rover's appearance?
(5) Why did the super decide at the beginning not to leave Rover to die alone in the desert?
(6) How did the dog react to being given the water?
(7) What were the super's daughter's feelings towards the dog?
(8) How did those at the station first know that Rover was dead?

Years ago, the swagmen trudging the dusty outback roads were said to be 'waltzing matilda', or carrying their swag. This poem tells what happens to one such swagman who steals a sheep from a squatter.

WALTZING MATILDA

Once a jolly swagman camped by a billabong,
    Under the shade of a coolabah tree,
And he sang as he watched and waited till his billy boiled,
    'Who'll come a-waltzing Matilda with me?
        Waltzing Matilda,
        Waltzing Matilda,
    Who'll come a-waltzing Matilda with me?'
And he sang as he watched and waited till his billy boiled,
    'Who'll come a-waltzing Matilda with me?'

Down came a jumbuck to drink at the billabong:
    Up jumped the swagman and grabbed him with glee.
And he sang as he shoved that jumbuck in his tucker-bag,
    'You'll come a-waltzing Matilda with me.
        Waltzing Matilda,
        Waltzing Matilda,
    You'll come a-waltzing Matilda with me.'

And he sang as he shoved that jumbuck in his tucker-bag,
  'You'll come a-waltzing Matilda with me.'

Up rode a squatter, mounted on his thoroughbred;
  Down came the troopers, one, two, three:
'Whose' that jolly jumbuck you've got in your tucker-bag?
  You'll come a-waltzing Matilda with me!
    Waltzing Matilda,
    Waltzing Matilda,
  You'll come a-waltzing Matilda with me.
Whose' that jolly jumbuck you've got in your tucker-bag?
  You'll come a-waltzing Matilda with me!'

Up jumped the swagman and sprang into the billagong;
  'You'll never catch me alive!' said he;
And his ghost may be heard as you pass by that billabong,
  'You'll come a-waltzing Matilda with me!
    Waltzing Matilda,
    Waltzing Matilda,
  You'll come a-waltzing Matilda with me!'
And his ghost may be heard as you pass by that billabong,
  'You'll come a-waltzing Matilda with me!'

A. B. ('BANJO') PATERSON

Waltzing Matilda — Coming to terms

Using the following explanations of some of the unusual words from the poem, describe in your own words what happens in 'Waltzing Matilda'.

SWAGMAN	A man who travelled on foot and carried his swag (possessions bundled in a blanket) slung across his back.
BILLABONG	A waterhole formed from a river system. The Aboriginal word meant 'dead water'.
BILLY (or billy-can)	A tin can with a wire handle and sometimes a lid. Australian bushmen used it as a kettle.
COOLABAH	A kind of gumtree, usually found along inland watercourses.
JUMBUCK	A sheep.
TUCKER-BAG	The bag in which the swagman carried his food.
SQUATTER	A landholder. (See also p. 17.)

3. Similes

The poet works with words, often putting them together so skilfully that they call up pictures in our minds. The poet might present us with something altogether familiar — a bird, an apple, the moon, an animal — and make us see it as we have never seen it before. One way that a poet can do this is by introducing a **simile**. The simile asks us to picture one thing as being *similar* to another; it does this by using the word 'like', 'as' or 'than'. Let us look at a few examples.

Some Similes

More than three and a half centuries ago the great poet and playwright William Shakespeare wrote a description of a young attractive woman, called Kate, in which he used three startling similes, one after the other. The lines (from *The Taming of the Shrew*, Act II, Scene 1) are quoted below. Can you identify these similes?

> Kate, like the hazel-twig,
> Is straight and slender; and as brown in hue
> As hazel-nuts, and sweeter than the kernels.

The poet and novelist D. H. Lawrence has used similes to give us his impression of bats. Find the similes in this extract from 'Bats':

> Wings like bits of umbrella.
> Bats!
> Creatures that hang themselves upside down
>   like an old rag to sleep.

In the following extract from 'Reynard the Fox', John Masefield, by his use of similes, emphasizes the speed of the fox as it endeavours to escape from the hunters. Write down the simile you liked best and explain why you liked it.

from REYNARD THE FOX

Like a rocket shot to a ship ashore
The lean red bolt of his body tore,
Like a ripple of wind running swift on grass;
Like a shadow on wheat when a cloud blows past,
Like a turn at the buoy in a cutter sailing
When the bright green gleam lips white at the railing,
Like the April snake whipping back to sheath,
Like the gannets' hurtle on fish beneath,
Like a kestrel chasing, like a sickle reaping,
Like all things swooping, like all things sweeping,
Like a hound for stay, like a stag for swift,
With his shadow beside like spinning drift.

JOHN MASEFIELD

Simile Poems

Write down the similes found in the four short poems that follow. Then, select one simile from each poem and say why you like or dislike it.

• CATERPILLAR

Like a snake with legs it moves
carefully like a waddling bridge.
It looks like a little green wire with legs.
It has humps like a camel.

MARTIN THORNTON

AN ABORIGINAL SIMILE

There was no stir among the trees,
No pulse in the earth,
No movement in the void;
The grass was a dry white fire.
Then in the distance rose a cloud,
And a swift rain came:
Like a woman running,
The wind in her hair.

MARY GILMORE

FIREWORKS

They rise like sudden fiery flowers
  That burst upon the night,
Then fall to earth in burning showers
  Of crimson, blue, and white.

Like buds too wonderful to name,
  Each miracle unfolds,
And catherine-wheels begin to flame
  Like whirling marigolds.

Rockets and Roman candles make
  An orchard of the sky,
Whence magic trees their petals shake
  Upon each gazing eye.

JAMES REEVES

SYMPHONY IN YELLOW

An omnibus across the bridge
   Crawls like a yellow butterfly,
   And, here and there, a passer-by
Shows like a little restless midge.

Big barges full of yellow hay
   Are moored against the shadowy wharf,
   And, like a yellow silken scarf,
The thick fog hangs along the quay.

The yellow leaves begin to fade
   And flutter from the Temple elms,
   And at my feet the pale green Thames
Lies like a rod of rippled jade.

OSCAR WILDE

Striking Similes

Similes are part of the everyday currency of speech. They make language richer and more vivid. See whether you can complete these everyday similes using the words in the box.

finger	eggs	Attila	golfballs	ants
seal	turkey	cobra	machine	lettuce
snowflake	fish	weasel	grave	rat

(1) They were as compatible as a mongoose and a ....

(2) He was as quick as a .... up a drainpipe.

(3) She had as much chance as a .... in Hell.

(4) His face was as stern as a well-kept ....

(5) They were as scared as a .... in November.

(6) They were as busy as .... at a picnic.

(7) You were blubbering like a ....

(8) He was as welcome as .... the Hun.

(9) It was as crisp as a young ....

(10) The carpet was so thick you could lose .... in it.

(11) His hand was as clammy as a wet ....

(12) She was as greedy as a .... in a hen-house.

(13) They got on together like ham and ....

(14) He fought like a threshing- ....

(15) She was dressed up like a sore ....

4. Folks and Family

You often hear how *other* folks' folks are funny/Ha-ha or funny/Peculiar. This poem certainly confirms it.

FOLKS

I've heard so much about other folks' folks,
How somebody's Uncle told such jokes
The cat split laughing and had to be stitched,
How somebody's Aunt got so bewitched
She fried the kettle and washed the water
And spanked a letter and posted her daughter.
Other folks' folks get so well known,
And nobody knows about my own.

TED HUGHES

Grandad's will revealed that he knew his family better than they knew him. He agreed that 'where there's a will, there's a way'— and he found the way!

WHERE THERE'S A WILL

... there's a sobbing relation

All the family was gathered
To hear poor Grandad's will,
Fred was watching Alice,
And she was watching Bill,
He was watching Arthur,
Everywhere he went,
But specially at the cupboard,
Where Grandad kept the rent.

Outside on the patio,
The sliding door was closed,
And sitting in a chair
Was nephew John, his face composed.
He said 'Me dear old Grandad,
I shall never see you more'
And his sheets of calculations
Were spread across the floor.

Downstairs in the kitchen,
Sister Alice blew her nose,
Saying 'He always was my favourite,
You *knew* that I suppose?
You couldn't have found a nicer man,
I've never loved one dearer,
I'd have come round *much* more often,
If I'd lived just that bit nearer.'

Cousin Arthur sat alone,
His eyes were wild and rash,
And desperately he tried to think
Where old folks hid their cash.
He'd thought about the armchair,
And the mattress on the bed,
And he'd left his car at home,
And booked a Pickfords van instead.

Then there were the bedroom floorboards,
He'd studied every crack,
And twice, while dusting the commode,
He'd rolled the carpet back,
But he knew the others watched him,
'You scavengers' he cursed,
And every night he prayed,
'Don't let the others find it first'.

The day that Grandad's will was read,
It came up bright and clear,
The solicitor looked round,
And said 'Now then, are we all here?'
Someone shouted 'Yes'
And someone else unscrewed his pen,
And someone sat upon his coat,
So he could not stand up again.

He carefully unfolded it
And wonderingly said,
'This is the shortest will
I ever will have read'.
He rolled a fag and carefully
Laid in a filter tip,
While beads of sweat they gathered
On Cousin Arthur's lip.

It says: 'Me dear relations,
Thank you all for being so kind,
And out beside the lily pond
You will surely find,
The half a million pounds
With which I stuffed me garden gnome,
Which I leave, with great affection,
To the Battersea Dogs' Home.'

PAM AYRES

Where There's a Will — Some questions
(1) Why was all the family gathered?
(2) Who went to the cupboard where Grandad kept the rent?
(3) How did nephew John reveal a contradictory attitude towards his dear old Grandad?
(4) Why was sister Alice a bit of a hypocrite?

(5) What did cousin Arthur desperately try to think?

(6) Why did Arthur leave his car at home and book a van instead?

(7) What did Arthur pray for every night?

(8) In your opinion, which of the relations was the most honest?

(9) Briefly describe what happened in the sixth stanza.

(10) What, to the solicitor, was strange about the will?

(11) What was happening to the cousin while the solicitor was taking his time over the will?

(12) Where was Grandad's money stuffed?

(13) Where, according to his will, would Grandad's money end up?

At first glance, the next poem is simply about a father who, all in fun, waltzes his small son round the kitchen. However, at second glance you pick up disturbing sensations and words: 'The whiskey on your breath', the small boy holding on 'like death' and the frown on the mother's face. Then there's the father's battered knuckle and his work-hardened hand beating time on the boy's head. Despite all this, the boy clings to his father as the father waltzes him off to bed.

MY PAPA'S WALTZ

The whiskey on your breath
Could make a small boy dizzy;
But I held on like death:
Such waltzing was not easy.

We romped until the pans
Slid from the kitchen shelf;
My mother's countenance
Could not unfrown itself.

The hand that held my wrist
Was battered on one knuckle;
At every step you missed
My right ear scraped a buckle.

You beat time on my head
With a palm caked hard by dirt,
Then waltzed me off to bed
Still clinging to your shirt.

THEODORE ROETHKE

Relax when you read the following poem because it's just for your enjoyment. You'll see that while the subject of the poem is peculiar, it is also particular — a father's thumb receives praise for the great deeds of strength it can perform around the home.

MY DAD'S THUMB

My dad's thumb
can stick pins in wood
without flinching —
it can crush family-size matchboxes
in one stroke
and lever off jam-jar lids without piercing
at the pierce here sign.

If it wanted
it could be a bath-plug
or a paint-scraper
a keyhole cover or a tap-tightener.

It's already a great nutcracker
and if it dressed up
it could easily pass
as a broad bean or a big toe.

In actual fact, it's quite simply
the world's fastest envelope burster.

MICHAEL ROSEN

Not all mothers cook — not all mothers *want* to cook. But this mother can
and does! Let Ted Hughes tell you how.

MY MOTHER

All mothers can serve up a bit of buttered toast,
Most mothers can handle a pie or a roast,
A few can boil a shark à la Barbary Coast,
But when I say mine can COOK — it's no boast.

When the Maharajah of old Srinigar
Wishes to make himself popular
Who can help him out but my Ma?
With elephant loads of nuts and suet,
With hundreds of coolies to trample through it
(To stir it you see), she produces a Cake
As huge as a palace that architects make —
Frosted and crusted with pink and blue icing.
Oh think of the knife they need for the slicing!

But special dishes are more to her wishes —
Nutritious, delicious, peculiar dishes —
Not just kippers in carrot juice,
But Buffalo Puff and Whipped-Cream Goose,
A Bouillabaisse out of no cook-book pages
With Whale and Walrus in collops and wedges
And festoons of Octopus over the edges.
(And should that give you the slightest uneasiness
There's Rose Crush topped with a peach's fleeciness.)

Sautéed Ant Eggs on Champagne Alligator
Are wonderful with a baked potato!
I took her a rattlesnake that had attacked us:
She served it up curried with Crème de la Cactus.

Her kitchen is a continual crisis,
Billowing clouds of aromas and spices —
Bubbling cauldrons and humming ovens,
Pans spitting by sixes, pots steaming by sevens.

Most mothers stick to their little cook-books,
But this is the way *my* Mother cooks!

TED HUGHES

My Mother — Stir a thought

(1)   What is the strangest piece of cooking mentioned in the first stanza?

(2)   What examples of exaggeration can you find in the second stanza? Why do you think the poet exaggerates?

(3)   What would be incredible about 'the knife they need for the slicing' of Ma's cake?

(4)   In the third stanza, three qualities found in Ma's special dishes are named. What are they?

(5)   What, in your opinion, is Ma's most exotic dish?

(6)   How did Ma serve up the rattlesnake?

(7)   If you were to enter Ma's kitchen, which is in a state of 'continual crisis', what would (a) pungently assault your nostrils? (b) harshly assault your ears?

(8)   How does the mother in the poem differ, in the matter of cooking, from most other mothers?

Next we have a poem concerned with the infuriating qualities possessed by wholemeal bread.

MY BROTHER IS MAKING A PROTEST ABOUT BREAD

My brother is making a protest about bread.
'Why do we always have wholemeal bread?
You can't spread the butter on wholemeal bread,
you try to spread the butter on
and it just makes a hole right through the middle.'

He marches out of the room and shouts
across the landing and down the passage.
'It's always the same in this place.
Nothing works.
The volume knob's broken on the radio you know,
it's been broken for months and months you know.'

He stamps back into the kitchen
stares at the loaf of bread and says:
'Wholemeal bread — look at it, look at it.
You put the butter on
and it all rolls up,
you put the butter on
and it all rolls up.'

MICHAEL ROSEN

This Lennon–McCartney song-poem is about a daughter leaving home.

SHE'S LEAVING HOME

Wednesday morning at five o'clock as the day begins,
Silently closing her bedroom door,
Leaving the note that she hoped would say more,
She goes downstairs to the kitchen
Clutching her handkerchief,
Quietly turning the backdoor key,
Stepping outside, she is free.
She (we gave her most of our lives)
is leaving (sacrificed most of our lives)
home (we gave her everything money could buy) —
She's leaving home after living alone
For so many years. Bye, bye.

Father snores as his wife gets into her dressing gown,
Picks up the letter that's lying there,
Standing alone at the top of the stairs
She breaks down and cries to her husband,
'Daddy, our baby's gone.
Why would she treat us so thoughtlessly?
How could she do this to me?'
She (we never thought of ourselves)
is leaving (never a thought for ourselves)
home (we struggled hard all our lives to get by) —
She's leaving home after living alone
For so many years. Bye, bye.

Friday morning by nine o'clock she is far away,
Waiting to keep the appointment she made,
Meeting a man from the motor trade,
She (what did we do that was wrong?)
is having (we didn't know it was wrong)
fun (fun is the one thing that money can't buy);
Something inside that was always denied
For so many years. Bye, bye.
She's leaving home. Bye, bye.

JOHN LENNON and **PAUL McCARTNEY**

She's Leaving Home — What went wrong?

(1)   What evidence can you find to suggest that the daughter has been crying?

(2)   Who do you think is speaking the words in the brackets?

(3)   'She's leaving home after living alone / For so many years.' There's a contradiction in these words. Can you explain it?

(4)   In your own words, sum up what happens in the second stanza.

(5)   In the last stanza we receive a clue as to why the daughter left home. What is the clue and why did she leave?

Discussion Point

Young people do leave home and, although most leave for good reasons, some leave 'under a cloud'. What, in your opinion, are good and proper reasons for leaving home? Contrast these with what you consider to be reasons for leaving home which will cause misunderstanding or bad feeling between parents and their children. In such cases, is it the parents or the children who are to blame?

'My Grandmother' is a poem that explores the bond between a person and her possessions. The person is the grandmother and her possessions are the things she kept in her antique shop.

We see the grandmother through the eyes of her granddaughter. The girl used to think of her grandmother as someone who had little need of love: the woman had surrounded herself with the antiques she cared for, and they in turn 'kept her'. Not wishing to be 'used' like one of these antiques, the granddaughter had once refused to go out with her. After that she always felt guilty because she knew she had misunderstood and hurt her grandmother, who was a woman of deep feeling after all.

The lesson that she had hurt and seriously misjudged another human being was brought home to the granddaughter as she watched her grandmother growing older and surrounding herself with the things she needed — not for the things themselves but for the memories of people which those things contained ('things she never used / But needed').

In the end, the granddaughter realized that her grandmother had taught her one of the great lessons of life — that appearances can be very deceptive.

MY GRANDMOTHER

She kept an antique shop — or it kept her.
Among Apostle spoons and Bristol glass,
The faded silks, the heavy furniture,
She watched her own reflection in the brass
Salvers and silver bowls, as if to prove
Polish was all, there was no need of love.

And I remember how I once refused
To go out with her, since I was afraid.
It was perhaps a wish not to be used
Like antique objects. Though she never said
That she was hurt, I still could feel the guilt
Of that refusal, guessing how she felt.

Later, too frail to keep a shop, she put
All her best things in one long narrow room;
The place smelt old, of things too long kept shut,
The smell of absences where shadows come
That can't be polished. There was nothing then
To give her own reflection back again.

And when she died I felt no grief at all,
Only the guilt of what I once refused.
I walked into her room among the tall
Sideboards and cupboards — things she never used
But needed; and no finger-marks were there,
Only the new dust falling through the air.

ELIZABETH JENNINGS

The grandpa portrayed in the next poem was an exceptional man. Read through the many skills he taught his grandchild, then learn what happened to grandpa when he grew old.

GRANDPA

Grandpa he was a man
he taught me the things that mattered
how to eat oxtail soup before
fishing on Saturday morning to
keep you warm how to
cast a line into a
streamful of angered anglers and
be the only one to
come home with anything worth
bragging about how to
set teeth in any saw and
dovetail a joint in a
chair leg and roof a
house and weld a
straight seam on a
kitchen pipe and make a
home out of a
workshop out of a
two-car garage and
smoke Granger's tobacco and
love work and kids and
fishing for 'a Man's
life is his work and
his work is his life' and
once you take away his work
you pull the plug of his life
and it takes too long
for it to drain silently away.
One day they came and
told him to go home and
rest old man it's time
that you retire he begged
them 'let me stay' but
they of course knew best for
everyone knows at sixty-five
all men are old and useless and
must be cast off to

rot so he came home and
tried to fish and
couldn't and tried to joke and
couldn't and tried to live and
couldn't. Every morning he was
up at four and cooked breakfast for
grandma and warmed up the house and
went to the workshop and
filed saws for neighbors but
they told him to stop that too
so he put all his tools away and
cleaned up the workshop and
came into the house for his
daily afternoon nap and
died. They didn't know
what I knew because he
didn't tell them but
he showed them
Grandpa he was a man.

W. M. RANSOM
(Northern Cheyenne Indian)

Grandpa — Thinking about the poem

(1) Which one of the following applies to 'the things that mattered' which Grandpa taught, as listed in the first twenty lines of the poem? (a) they were all of help with schoolwork (b) they were to do with jobs around the house (c) they were all practical.
(2) How did Grandpa link a man's life with his work?
(3) When Grandpa was talking about taking away a man's work, what comparison did he make?
(4) 'One day they came....' Can you suggest who *they* might have been?
(5) In the part of the poem which deals with Grandpa being forcibly retired, what bitter words are used?
(6) How did Grandpa ultimately show them he was a man?

More Thinking

Think about each of the following:
(1) What *do* the elderly have to offer to younger people in a society?
(2) In what unfeeling, uncaring ways are the elderly often treated by those with whom they live?
(3) What responsibilities are owed by society to its elderly? Why?

Some Ruthless Relatives

SISTER NELL

In the family drinking well
Willie pushed his sister Nell.
She's there yet, because it kilt her —
Now we have to buy a filter.

POLITENESS

My cousin John was most polite;
He led shortsighted Mrs Bond,
By accident, one winter's night
Into a village pond.
Her life perhaps he might have saved
But how genteelly he behaved!

Each time she rose and waved to him
He smiled and bowed and doffed his hat;
Thought he, although I cannot swim,
At least I can do that —
And when for the third time she sank
He stood bareheaded on the bank.

Be civil, then, to young and old;
Especially to persons who
Possess a quantity of gold
Which they might leave to you.
The more they have, it seems to me,
The more polite you ought to be.

HARRY GRAHAM

YOUNG SAMMY WATKINS

Young Sammy Watkins jumped out of bed;
He ran to his sister and cut off her head.
This gave his dear mother a great deal of pain;
She hopes that he never will do it again.

GRAN

I came from the bush with my Gran
At Bourke Street we got off a tram
   DON'T WALK the sign said
   'Goodness gracious,' Gran said.
Then she kicked off her shoes and ran.

FATHER AND SON

When Father took out his new car,
His son, who was with him, cried 'Pa,
   If you drive at this rate
   We are sure to be *late*.
Drive faster!' He did, and they are!

MY SISTER LAURA

My sister Laura's bigger than me
And lifts me up quite easily.
I can't lift her, I've tried and tried;
She must have something heavy inside.

SPIKE MILLIGAN

LIZZIE BORDEN WITH AN AXE

Lizzie Borden with an axe
Hit her father forty whacks,
When she saw what she had done,
She hit her mother forty-one.

UNCLE

Uncle, whose inventive brains
Kept evolving aeroplanes,
Fell from an enormous height
On my garden lawn, last night.
Flying is a fatal sport,
Uncle wrecked the tennis-court.

HARRY GRAHAM

5. Metaphors

The **metaphor** takes us a step further than the simile. Instead of asking us to picture one thing as *being like* another, we are asked to picture one thing as *being* another.

* My love is like a red, red rose. (SIMILE)
* My love is a red, red rose. (METAPHOR)

Everyday Metaphors

We regularly use metaphors in our everyday speech. Many of these metaphors are used so often that they, unlike those of the poet, have lost much of their original spontaneity. Even so, they still can express our meaning more forcefully than a literal statement. Look at the following sentences, which contain everyday metaphors. Then explain the meaning of each of the sentences.

Colour Metaphors
(1) The teacher gave the student a *black* look.
(2) Out of the *blue*, our relatives arrived.
(3) We've been given the *green* light to go ahead with the project.
(4) The burglar was caught *red*-handed.
(5) The boy told his mother a *white* lie.

Food Metaphors
(1) He had a *plum* job.
(2) I didn't have a *bean* to spend.
(3) She was the *apple* of her father's eye.
(4) The student's insolence landed him in the *soup*.
(5) The boxer made *mincemeat* of his opponent.

Weather Metaphors
(1) The police are in a *fog* about the robbery.
(2) The receptionist gave the enquirer a *frosty* glance.
(3) Her wealth cuts no *ice* here.
(4) The union called a *lightning* strike.
(5) The headmaster was *snowed* under with work.

Three Metaphor Poems

The metaphors of the poet enable us to see commonplace objects with a fresh and often startling vision. How many of us would think of a toaster as a silver-scaled dragon?

THE TOASTER

A silver-scaled Dragon with jaws flaming red
Sits at my elbow and toasts my bread.
I hand him fat slices, and then, one by one,
He hands them back when he sees they are done.

WILLIAM JAY SMITH

In the next poem, 'Steam Shovel', the poet's imagination and powers of observation work in unison as the steam shovel he observes becomes an amiable dinosaur feeding on earth and grass.

STEAM SHOVEL

The dinosaurs are not all dead.
I saw one raise its iron head
To watch me walking down the road
Beyond our house today.
Its jaws were dripping with a load
Of earth and grass that it had cropped.
It must have heard me where I stopped,
Snorted white steam my way,
And stretched its long neck out to see,
And chewed, and grinned quite amiably.

CHARLES MALAM

Perhaps some of us, like the poet Beatrice Janosco, have imagined that our garden hose is really a serpent drinking from the garden tap.

THE GARDEN HOSE

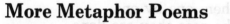

In the grey evening
I see a long green serpent
With its tail in the dahlias.

It lies in loops across the grass
And drinks softly at the faucet.

I can hear it swallow.

BEATRICE JANOSCO

More Metaphor Poems

The effect of twentieth-century living is seen in 'Subway' and 'Tree Poem'.

SUBWAY

Every day I step into a coffin
with strangers.

Nailing hurriedly
my own coffin.

I go toward the city
to be buried alive.

ETSURO SAKAMOTO

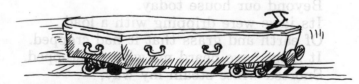

Subway — Metaphor questions
(1) Why is the poet's comparison of the subway to a coffin appropriate?
(2) What other words continue the poet's coffin image?

Here's a most unexpected metaphor. The poet William Hart-Smith compares a tree to a factory.

from TREE POEM

A tree
Is a factory manufacturing
long polymer molecules
with a
tall
chimney
spewing forth
the breath
of life
as a waste product.

W. HART-SMITH

Tree Poem — Metaphor questions

(1) What do you think the 'tall chimney' is?
(2) What is the 'waste product'?

The writer of 'Apartment House' uses the combination of metaphor and simile to convey his feelings about living in an apartment block.

APARTMENT HOUSE

A filing-cabinet of human lives
Where people swarm like bees in tunneled hives,
Each to his own cell in the towered comb,
Identical and cramped — we call it home.

GERALD RAFTERY

Apartment House — Metaphor questions

(1) 'A filing-cabinet of human lives' is a metaphor that suggests something about the apartment house. What?
(2) What picture of the apartment house do you gain from the simile 'like bees in tunneled hives'?

In the following poem, James Reeves's imagination and his acute perception have transformed the sea into a hungry dog.

THE SEA

The sea is a hungry dog.
Giant and grey.
He rolls on the beach all day.
With his clashing teeth and shaggy jaws

Hour upon hour he gnaws
The rumbling, tumbling stones,
And 'Bones, bones, bones, bones!'
The giant sea-dog moans,
Licking his greasy paws.

And when the night wind roars
And the moon rocks in the stormy cloud,
He bounds to his feet and snuffs and sniffs,
Shaking his wet sides over the cliffs,
And howls and hollos long and loud.

But on quiet days in May or June,
When even the grasses on the dune
Play no more their reedy tune,
With his head between his paws
He lies on the sandy shores,

So quiet, so quiet, he scarcely snores.

JAMES REEVES

The Sea — The poet's craft

(1) The whole poem is a metaphor. What two things are being identified?
(2) 'Giant and grey.' What two qualities of the sea is James Reeves emphasizing?
(3) What are some of the qualities the sea and a dog have in common?
(4) Can you suggest why the poet writes 'bones' four times in the one line?

(5) 'Shaking his wet sides over the cliffs . . . .' What is the sea doing?

(6) 'And howls and hollos long and loud.' What aspect of the sea is the poet emphasizing?

(7) 'With his head between his paws . . . .' What does this dog-picture indicate about the sea?

(8) In the last two lines of the poem, the poet uses quite a number of 's' sounds. What picture of the sea do these sounds give you?

Identify the metaphor in this 'BC' cartoon. In your own words, explain what it means.

6. Chalk and Talk

TEACHER, TEACHER

Teacher, teacher, don't be dumb!
Give me back my bubble gum!

Teacher, teacher, I declare,
Tarzan lost his underwear!

Teacher, teacher, don't be mean,
Give me a dime for the coke machine!

TRADITIONAL

And then the whining schoolboy, with his satchel
And shining morning face, creeping like snail
Unwillingly to school.

WILLIAM SHAKESPEARE
(As You Like It, II, vii)

Here's a poem that treats a very familiar situation. Just when you think you've got to know your teacher and all her faults, and to appreciate exactly what you can get away with, she ups and leaves and there appears a fearsome replacement!

OUR NEW TEACHER

This teacher has such scary teeth,
they look just like a shark's;
His eyes gleam in the sunlight
like a pair of purple sparks.
His voice is just as booming
as the roar from some big gun;
He can imitate a thunderstorm
for a gruesome bit of fun.
And now Billy who was silly
almost every other day
Does his tables, writes his spellings,
hides his comic book away.
Every lesson lasts a lifetime . . .
with our noses to each page,
We imagine bars on windows
and the classroom seems a cage.

So, please come back, Miss Fothergill:
though you won't believe it's true,
We all loved you as our teacher;
we were oh, so fond of you!

DAVID BATESON

Our New Teacher — Reading for detail

(1) What does the simile 'like a shark's' suggest about the appearance of the new teacher's teeth?
(2) Give the word that tells us how his eyes looked in the sunlight.
(3) What word accurately describes the sound of the new teacher's voice?
(4) How does the silly Billy of the past compare with the Billy under the control of the new teacher?
(5) How long does every lesson seem to last under the new teacher?
(6) What plea is uttered in the closing stanza?

Read 'Sick' and laugh at the inventiveness of Peggy Ann McKay. She cannot go to school, and the reason is every symptom and 'sickness' under the sun — from 'my eyes are blue' to 'instamatic flu'. As you approach the end of the poem, look out for Peggy's miraculous and unexpected recovery.

SICK

'I cannot go to school today,'
Said little Peggy Ann McKay.
'I have the measles and the mumps,
A gash, a rash and purple bumps.
My mouth is wet, my throat is dry,
I'm going blind in my right eye.
My tonsils are as big as rocks,
I've counted sixteen chicken pox
And there's one more — that's seventeen,
And don't you think my face looks green?
My leg is cut, my eyes are blue —
It might be instamatic flu.
I cough and sneeze and gasp and choke,
I'm sure that my left leg is broke —
My hip hurts when I move my chin,
My belly button's caving in,
My back is wrenched, my ankle's sprained,
My 'pendix pains each time it rains.
My nose is cold, my toes are numb,
I have a sliver in my thumb,
My neck is stiff, my spine is weak,
I hardly whisper when I speak.
My tongue is filling up my mouth,
I think my hair is falling out.
My elbow's bent, my spine ain't straight,
My temperature is one-o-eight.
My brain is shrunk, I cannot hear,
There is a hole inside my ear.
I have a hangnail, and my heart is — what?
What's that? What's that you say?
You say today is ... Saturday?
G'bye, I'm going out to play!'

SHEL SILVERSTEIN

The student in the following poem has a desk at the back of the class where he or she leads a secret existence as a Marrog. The poem runs through the physical appearance of the Marrog, then turns to the extraordinary powers it possesses, and finally deals with the devastating effects the Marrog would have on the class if its monstrous presence in their midst were suddenly discovered.

THE MARROG

My desk's at the back of the class
And nobody nobody knows
I'm a Marrog from Mars
With a body of brass
And seventeen fingers and toes.
Wouldn't they shriek if they knew
I've three eyes at the back of my head
And my hair is bright purple
My nose is deep blue
And my teeth are half yellow half red?
My five arms are silver with knives on them sharper than spears.
I could go back right now if I liked —
And return in a million light years.
I could gobble them all for
I'm seven foot tall
And I'm breathing green flames from my ears.
Wouldn't they yell if they knew
If they guessed that a Marrog was here?
Ha-ha they haven't a clue —
Or wouldn't they tremble with fear!
Look, look, a Marrog
They'd all scrum and shout.
The blackboard would fall and the ceiling would crack
And the teacher would faint I suppose.
But I grin to myself sitting right at the back
And nobody nobody knows.

R. C. SCRIVEN

The Marrog — A spotter's guide
Identify the Marrog by drawing up the following MARROG IDENTIFICATION CHART in your workbook and completing it according to vital information supplied in the poem. (The first piece of information is supplied.)

MARROG IDENTIFICATION CHART

BACKGROUND

1	Where Marrog Usually Lurks in a Classroom	*at the back*
2	Planet of Origin	

PHYSICAL

1	Composition of Body	
2	Number of Fingers + Toes	
3	Number of Eyes	
4	Position of Eyes	
5	Colour of Hair	
6	Colour of Nose	
7	Colour of Teeth	
8	Colour and Number of Arms	
9	Height	

WEAPONS

1	Arms Armed with	
2	Ears Produce	

PROBABLE DEVASTATING EFFECTS ON OTHERS IF/WHEN MARROG APPEARS

1	Fellow Students Would All	
2	Blackboard Would	
3	Ceiling Would	
4	Teacher Would	

IDENTIKIT PICTURE: Draw a frame and, from the information contained in the above chart, produce your own Identikit picture of the MARROG. Display this in a prominent position beneath your chart so that all may be warned!

'The ABC' is a fun poem by Spike Milligan which brings to life, on the stroke of midnight in the schoolroom, some lively letters of the alphabet.

THE ABC

'Twas midnight in the schoolroom
And every desk was shut,
When suddenly from the alphabet
Was heard a loud 'Tut-tut!'

Said A to B, 'I don't like C;
His manners are a lack.
For all I ever see of C
Is a semi-circular back!'

'I disagree,' said D to B,
'I've never found C so.
From where I stand, he seems to be
An uncompleted O.'

C was vexed, 'I'm much perplexed,
You criticize my shape.
I'm made like that, to help spell Cat
And Cow and Cool and Cape.'

'He's right,' said E; said F, 'Whoopee!'
Said G, ' 'Ip, 'ip, 'ooray!'
'You're dropping me,' roared H to G.
'Don't do it please I pray!'

'Out of my way,' L said to K.
'I'll make poor I look ILL.'
To stop this stunt, J stood in front,
And presto! ILL was JILL.

'U know,' said V, 'that W
Is twice the age of me,
For as a Roman V is five
I'm half as young as he.'

X and Y yawned sleepily,
'Look at the time!' they said.
'Let's all get off to beddy byes.'
They did, then, 'Z-z-z.'

alternative last verse:

X and Y yawned sleepily,
'Look at the time!' they said.
They all jumped in to beddy byes
And the last one in was Z!

ZZZZZ

Z

SPIKE MILLIGAN

The schoolgirl in the next poem is made up of all the things she experiences — the things she sees, hears, feels, smells, tastes, remembers — all that she has been taught and all that she thinks. She is wrapped in a cocoon of experience composed of the good and bad things of the past and present. But one day she'll free herself of this cocoon and emerge as a woman.

WOMAN OF THE FUTURE

I am a child.
I am all the things of my past.
I am the freckles from my mother's nose.
I am the laziness of my dad
    Resting his eyes in front of the television.
I am all I see.
    Boys doing Karate Chops.
    Rubens' lovely ladies,
    Fat and bulging.
    TV ads of ladies who wear lipstick in the laundry.
    And worry about their hands
    And their breath.
    Madonnas with delicate faces holding little bundles of Jesus.
I am all I hear.
    'Look after him. You're his sister.'
    'Come and get your hair done.'
    'Rack off, Normie!'
    Waves lapping or crashing at the beach.
    And the wind in trees and telegraph wires.
I am all I feel and taste.
    Soft and glossy mud on toes.
    Hairy insect legs
    Slippery camphor laurel leaves
    The salty taste of fish and chips on my tongue
    And the watery melting of iceblocks.

And all I remember.
  A veranda shaded by grape vines,
  Where I stepped off the edge and flew
  Like Superman.
  And waking up in the cold in a car where dad changed a tyre.
  And being lost in the zoo with my cousin.
I am all I've been taught.
  'I' before 'E' except after 'C'.
  'Smoking is a health hazard.'
I am all I think.
  Secrets.
  Deep down inside me.
I am all those things.
I'm like a caterpillar
And these things are my cocoon.
But one day I'll bite my way out
  And be free
  Because
I'm the woman of the future.

CATHY WARRY

Woman of the Future — Experiences checklist

Give one or two examples from the poem to illustrate each of the following areas of experience. The first one has been done to give you the idea.

AREAS OF EXPERIENCE

Violence
- *boys doing Karate Chops*
- ....

Feeling
- ....
- ....

Learnt at School
- ....
- ....

Advertisements
- ....

Heredity
- ....
- ....

Tastes
- ....
- ....

A Pleasant Memory
- ....

An Unpleasant Memory
- ....

A Responsibility
- ....

Beauty (with Humour)
- ....

Religion
- ....

Natural Sounds
- ....

Woman of the Future — Questions of simile

(1) Towards the end of the poem, a startling simile creates a comparison that helps you to picture the change from child to adult. Give the simile and explain the comparison that it draws.

(2) What other example of simile can you find in the poem?

Your turn to emerge

Using the poem 'Woman of the Future' as a model, write down the following 'I am ...' lines. Then, compose an original poem that draws upon experiences *of your own*. Close your 'I am ...' poem with a simile that is different from Cathy Warry's but still advances the idea of *emergence*.

I AM . . .

I am all I see.

....

....

I am all I hear.

....

....

I am all I feel.

....

....

I am all I taste.

....

....

I am all I remember.

....

....

I am all I've been taught.

....

....

I am all I think.

....

....

I am like ....

But ....

....

....

I am the ....

The clear, cool song of a bird breaks through the listless boredom of students mesmerized by the drone of the teacher's voice.

BIRD IN THE CLASSROOM

The students drowsed and drowned
In the teacher's ponderous monotone —
Limp bodies looping in the wordy heat,
Melted and run together, desks and flesh as one,
Swooning and swimming in a sea of drone.

Each one asleep, swayed and vaguely drifted
With lidding eyes and lolling, weighted heads,
Was caught on heavy waves and dimly lifted,
Sunk slowly, ears ringing, in the syrup of his sound,
Or borne from the room on a heaving wilderness of beds

And then, on a sudden, a bird's cool voice
Punched out song. Crisp and spare
On the startled air,
Beak-beamed
Or idly tossed,
Each note gleamed
Like a bead of frost.

A bird's cool voice from a neighbour tree
With five clear calls — mere grains of sound
Rare and neat
Repeated twice . . .
But they sprang the heat
Like drops of ice.

Ears cocked, before the comment ran
Fading and chuckling where a wattle stirred,
The students wondered how they could have heard
Such dreary monotones from man,
Such wisdom from a bird.

COLIN THIELE

In the following poem, we peer fearfully through the eyes of someone just starting school and discover how much there is that simply doesn't make sense.

FIRST DAY AT SCHOOL

A millionbillionwillion miles from home
Waiting for the bell to go. (To go where?)
Why are they all so big, other children?
So noisy? So much at home they
must have been born in uniform.
Lived all their lives in playgrounds.
Spent the years inventing games
that don't let me in. Games
that are rough, that swallow you up.

And the railings.
All around, the railings.
Are they to keep out wolves and monsters?
Things that carry off and eat children?
Things you don't take sweets from?
Perhaps they're to stop us getting out.
Running away from the lessins. Lessin.
What does a lessin look like?
Sounds small and slimy.
They keep them in glassrooms.
Whole rooms made out of glass. Imagine.

I wish I could remember my name.
Mummy said it would come in useful.
Like wellies. When there's puddles.*
Yellowwellies. I wish she was here.
I think my name is sewn on somewhere.
Perhaps the teacher will read it for me.
Tea-cher. The one who makes the tea.

ROGER McGOUGH

* Wellies are Wellingtons — rubber boots that reach the knee.

First Day at School — Responding to the poem

(1) In what way does the first line tell us that the new student is quite young?

(2)   Even the school bell adds to the child's confusion. What kind of confusion does he or she feel about the bell?

(3)   Explain in your own words why the other children appear so strange, so formidable and so organized.

(4)   In the second stanza of the poem, we see two things through the eyes of the new pupil: the railings round the school and the 'lessins'. What two possible uses for the railings does the child imagine?

(5)   Where might 'lessins' be kept?

(6)   What is very childlike about the child's use of a name?

(7)   Why does the child compare his/her name to a pair of 'wellies'?

(8)   What does the new pupil's imagination do with the word 'teacher'?

Some factories produce cars, other factories produce washing-machines. But all schools produce words — and words and freedom are what the next poem is all about.

In the first stanza, we find the formal 'well-dressed' words of the classroom filing from the teacher's lips to be noted attentively by the students. In the second stanza, words are out in the playground and running wild along with those who use them. In the last stanza, we come across a situation in which words would only get in the way.

FREEDOM OF SPEECH

The teacher's dry tone
dressed words in Sunday best
and droned them in rigid file to the students
who dutifully plucked them from the air
and skewered them with thick black strokes
in between the perfectly straight lines on the page.

It was the siren blasting out from the silver speaker on the wall
that allowed them to escape.
They flew out on the backs of shrieking yells
into the playground
where they quickly became delinquent,
breaking into brazen four-letter hops
and back-slapping each other with breezy buddy-calls
while they somersaulted with practised glee
into deliberate mispronunciations.

Only at the far corner of the yard
did they stop their jesting;
there where the young boy and girl stood
against a sun-warm wall,
arms encircling arms
foreheads touching,
Wordless.

VAL KOSTIC

Freedom of Speech — Working with words

(1) Explain, in your own words, 'The teacher's dry tone / dressed words in Sunday best'.

(2) What word well represents the monotonous sound of the teacher's dictating voice?

(3) What were the students doing with the teacher's words?

(4) What allowed the students to escape from the classroom?

(5) When the poet says 'They flew out on the backs of shrieking yells / into the playground', what kind of colourful picture is created in your mind?

(6) In the middle of the poem you come across the word 'delinquent'. What is the meaning of the word here in the poem? How does this meaning differ from the usual meaning of the word?

(7) The poet manages to link the carefree way the students move about in the playground with freedom of speech. How does the poet manage to connect movement and speech? (Quote from the poem if you like.)

(8) In the last stanza, why did the young boy and girl stand wordless?

(9) What is the double-meaning suggested by the title of the poem?

(10) Do you think the poem gives a true picture of school life? Why?

Kid Stuff

TOMATO JUICE

An accident happened to my brother Jim
When somebody threw a tomato at him —
Tomatoes are juicy and don't hurt the skin,
But this one was specially packed in a tin.

TOO MUCH

A greedy small lassie once said,
As she gobbled down slices of bread,
'If I eat one more crust,
I'm sure I will bust' —
At which point everyone fled.

A NUISANCE AT HOME

Bill learned to play tunes on a comb
And became such a nuisance at homb,
  That Ma spanked him and said
  'Shall I put you to baid?'
And he cheerfully answered her, 'Nomb'.

AGAIN

Jennie sat in a quiet nook
And wrote her name in a nice new book.
She wrote it down with a fountain pen
And when she had done it she wrote it again.

TABLES

Gertie Gables learnt her tables
Though it took her long.
Every night she got them right
Next day she got them wrong.

HOW SAD

There's a pitiful story — ah, me!
Of a young English girl named Nellie,
Who stared dumbly all day at TV
(Which in England is known as 'the telly') —
She died . . . and the reason, you see,
Was her brains had all turned into jelly!

WILLIAM COLE

7. Personification

Personification is a special kind of metaphor in which human characteristics are given to non-human things. You'll soon see what personification is as you look closely at this little poem about the wind by James Stephens. Notice how the wind becomes a person — a kind of wild man — who whistles, kicks, thumps and even wants to kill.

THE WIND

The wind stood up and gave a shout;
He whistled on his fingers, and

Kicked the withered leaves about,
And thumped the branches with his hand,

And said he'd kill, and kill, and kill;
And so he will! And so he will.

JAMES STEPHENS

In 'A Tree', the tree becomes human as it puts on or takes off the necessary clothing for each season.

A TREE

In Spring I look gay,
Decked in comely array,
In Summer more clothing I wear;
When colder it grows
I fling off my clothes,
And in Winter quite naked appear.

Now read through 'Snow'. Explain how, in their different ways, the fenceposts, the bushes and the trees have been personified.

SNOW

The fenceposts wear marshmallow hats
On a snowy day;
Bushes in their night gowns
Are kneeling down to pray —
And all the trees have silver skirts
And want to dance away.

DOROTHY ALDIS

'Tea Talk' is a humorous poem by C. J. Dennis. The tea things come to life, but they don't all have pleasant personalities.

TEA TALK

'Excuse me if I sit on you,' the cup said to the saucer.
  'I fear I've been here all the afternoon.'
'Spare excuses,' said the saucer; 'you have sat on me before, sir.'
  'Oh, I'll stir him up directly,' said the spoon.
'Stop your clatter! Stop your clatter!' cried the bread-and-butter
    platter.
  'Tittle-tattle!' sneered the tea-pot, with a shrug;
'Now, the most important question is my chronic indigestion.'
  'Ah, you've taken too much tannin,' jeered the jug.
'Hey, hey, hey!' sang the silver-plated tray,
'It's time you had your faces washed. I've come to clear away!'

C. J. DENNIS

Tea Talk — Identifying human qualities

Complete the following table by explaining how each of the tea objects has been personified. You may like to quote words from the poem as evidence.

OBJECT	HUMAN CHARACTERISTICS AND ACTIONS
Cup	
Saucer	
Spoon	
Bread-and-butter platter	
Tea-pot	
Jug	
Silver-plated tray	

In 'The Windmill', written more than a hundred years ago by Henry Wadsworth Longfellow, the windmill becomes a person of great size and strength — a giant.

THE WINDMILL

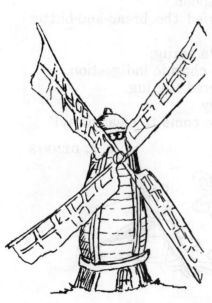

Behold! a giant am I!
  Aloft here in my tower,
  With my granite jaws I devour
The maize and the wheat and the rye,
  And grind them into flour.

I look down over the farms;
  In the fields of grain I see
  The harvest that is to be,
And I fling to the air my arms,
  For I know it is all for me.

I hear the sound of flails
  Far off, from the threshing-floors
  In barns, with their open doors,
And the wind, the wind in my sails,
  Louder and louder roars.

I stand here in my place,
With my foot on the rock below,
And whichever way it may blow
I meet it face to face,
As a brave man meets his foe.

And while we wrestle and strive,
My master, the miller, stands
And feeds me with his hands;
For he knows who makes him thrive,
Who makes him lord of lands.

On Sundays I take my rest;
Church-going bells begin
Their low, melodious din;
I cross my arms on my breast,
And all is peace within.

HENRY WADSWORTH LONGFELLOW

The Windmill — Finding personification

(1) In the first stanza, what human characteristic has the poet given the windmill?

(2) In the second stanza, what human things does the windmill do?

(3) In the third stanza, what human faculty has the windmill acquired?

(4) What, in human terms, is the windmill's relationship with the miller in the fifth stanza?

(5) In the last stanza, what actions of the windmill suggest that it is human?

Some famous poets speak

Each of the following examples of personification has been taken from a poem by a famous poet. See whether you can explain how the things in heavy type have been given human qualities.

(1)   The **pine trees** bend to listen to the autumn wind. ('At the Window' by D. H. Lawrence)

(2)   **Machine-guns** chuckled . . . / And the **Big Gun** guffawed. ('The Last Laugh' by Wilfred Owen)

(3)   The **leaves** fly over the window and utter a word as they pass. ('At the Window' by D. H. Lawrence)

(4)   And the **moonbeams** kiss the sea. ('Love's Philosophy' by Percy Bysshe Shelley)

(5)   The **black poplars** shake with hysterical laughter. ('At the Window' by D. H. Lawrence)

(6)   And the **waves** clasp one another. ('Love's Philosophy' by Percy Bysshe Shelley)

(7)   And the **sun** from sleep awaking, / Started up and said, 'Behold me!' ('Hiawatha's Sailing' by Henry Wadsworth Longfellow)

(8)   Where the **winds** are all asleep. ('The Forsaken Merman' by Matthew Arnold)

(9)   That orbéd maiden with white fire laden, / Whom mortals call the **moon**. ('The Cloud' by Percy Bysshe Shelley)

(10)   Boldly they rode and well, / Into the jaws of **Death**, / Into the mouth of **Hell** / Rode the six hundred. ('The Charge of the Light Brigade' by Alfred, Lord Tennyson)

8. The World of Animals

In 'Foxes among the Lambs,' the poet shares with us his reaction to the death of his lambs and his decision to poison the foxes responsible. The poet's description of his listening for the death-cries of the foxes is one the reader will not easily forget.

FOXES AMONG THE LAMBS

Each morning there were lambs with bloody mouth,
Their tongues cut out by foxes. Behind trees,
Where they had sheltered from the rainy South,
They'd rise to run, but fall on wobbly knees.
And knowing, though my heart was sick,
That only death could cure them of their ills,
I'd smash their heads in with handy stick
And curse the red marauders from the hills.

Each afternoon, safe in a sheltered nook
Behind the smithy, I'd prepare the bait;
And I remember how my fingers shook
With the half-frightened eagerness of hate
Placing the strychnine in the hidden rift
Made with the knife-point in the piece of liver;
And I would pray some fox would take my gift
And eat and feel the pinch and curse the giver.

Each night I'd lay abed sleepless until,
Above the steady patter of the rain,
I'd hear the first sharp yelp below the hill
And listen breathless till it rang again,
Nearer this time; then silence for a minute
While something in me waited for the leap
Of a wild cry with death and terror in it;
And then — it strikes me strange now — I could sleep!

ERNEST G. MOLL

Foxes among the Lambs — Sympathizing with the poet?

(1) 'I'd smash their heads in with handy stick ....' Why does the poet do this to the lambs?

(2) Who are the red marauders from the hills?

(3) Why would the foxes 'curse the giver' (i.e. the poet)?

(4) What words suggest the suffering of the foxes?

(5) 'I could sleep!' Why do you think the poet could sleep?

(6) Do you agree with what the poet did to the foxes? Why or why not?

(7) From your reading of the poem, what did you learn about the character of the poet?

Feelings

(1) What are the poet's feelings towards the lambs?

(2) What are the poet's feelings towards the foxes?

If you have ever had a possum trapped in the roof of your house, you'll know that the incessant noise of the animal trying to escape will spur you to action to release it, so that you can have peace and quiet again. Unfortunately this doesn't happen for the trapped old possum in the following poem, and the inside of the roof of the poet's house becomes the possum's tomb. Can you suggest why the possum failed to make its escape?

OLD MAN POSSUM

We did not know that you were dying old man possum
Among the rafters of the veranda roof
Trapped — if you had only whined or cried
As a cat would have cried, but you did not, for you
Said nothing, only perhaps shuffled over the rafters
Once or twice. And we failed to notice.
And only when you were long dead did we know
When the flies were angry.
                          We carried you deep down
To the bottom of the garden among the gumtrees,
Your ancestors' first home, and buried you
A large and uncouth ginger-coloured corpse
Grown old with eating berries and scraps and fighting,
Beneath the trees down in the damp clay.

And you had died trapped in the veranda roof,
Between the wood ceiling and the galvanised iron,
For one hot starlit night you must have come
To our veranda roof and had a look in
And pressing down a board that blocked your entry
Plunged into the gloom never to return ...
For when you tried to leave you found that the board
When you pulled it back and tried to climb over
Sprang upright. And you were trapped hopelessly
Beneath galvanised iron where no stars shone.

Days of being cooped in stifling air, thirsting,
Days of growing weakness growing hunger
You must have spent in there baked by the sun
Beating on the old roof, dazzled in your world
Of darkness by the fierce green line of garden
Creeping in from the edges of the roof.
Shambling stumbling about there helplessly
With your great heavy ugly scarred body.
And you bit a hole big enough to get through,
You bit a hole through a full inch of wood,
You bit a hole at the edge of the roof hoping ...
And when you had bitten it you found
That the overhanging galvanised iron blocked you
And you could only make scratch marks in the rust.

If you had only bitten through the board
Which stopped you getting out in the beginning ...
But you were to die in your animal stupidity.
If you had only bitten through the ceiling
On which you stood — and that was easily done —
You could have just jumped and dropped to freedom.
But through primeval instinct you never thought
Of moving earthwards — your race had always climbed.
And so you groped up to reach the sky and escape
From darkness and if you had only thought of the ground
You would have been saved. And so many die trying
To reach the sky, to escape from darkness, and if
They only thought of the ground they would be saved.

GEOFFREY LEHMANN

Sometimes it is more humane to put down a faithful animal that has been seriously injured than to allow it to endure its suffering. Such is the case in the poem below. Can you suggest why the poet has called his poem 'Last Run'?

LAST RUN

He'd fallen over a cliff
And he'd broken his leg.
Just a mustering dog.
And he looked at me, there on the hill,
Showing no hurt, as if he'd taken no ill,
And his ears, and his tail,
And his dark eyes too,
Said plainly,
'Well, Boss, what do we do?
Any more sheep to head?
Give me a run.'
But he'd never head sheep any more.

His day was done.
He thought it was fun
When I lifted the gun.

BRUCE STRONACH

What are your feelings about animals being kept in a zoo? Rainer Maria Rilke's description of the caged panther presents a convincing argument against the keeping of wild animals in captivity.

THE PANTHER

His weary glance, from passing by the bars,
Has grown into a dazed and vacant stare;
It seems to him there are a thousand bars
And out beyond those bars the empty air.

The pad of his strong feet, that ceaseless sound
Of supple tread beyond the iron bands,
Is like a dance of strength circling around,
While in the circle, stunned, a great will stands.

But there are times the pupils of his eyes
Dilate, the strong limbs stand alert, apart,
Tense with the flood of visions that arise
Only to sink and die within his heart.

RAINER MARIA RILKE
(translated from the German by Jessie Lamont)

The Panther — Questions to think about
(1) What is the poem about?
(2) Why is the panther's glance weary? What words continue this idea?
(3) What words indicate that the panther feels completely caged in?
(4) What words show the ceaseless movement of the panther?
(5) What words suggest that the panther is a powerful animal?
(6) What do you think 'the flood of visions' could be?
(7) The poem ends in despair. Explain why this is so.
(8) What would be another suitable title for this poem?

In 'Trapped Dingo', Judith Wright tells of a dead she-dingo she found caught in a trap on her country property. She reveals how she was overcome by its death. Not long before, the she-dingo's mate had been killed and the she-dingo had mourned him.

The poet uses the legend of Troy to evoke a feeling of sadness at the battle between the dingoes and their human adversaries. According to legend, Hector of Troy was slain by a Greek, Achilles, who dragged Hector's body three times around the walls of Troy. Hector's wife, Andromache, watching this tragic scene from the walls of Troy, was beside herself with grief. Later, when Troy fell, she too was killed by the Greeks. But the gods did not allow the killing of Hector by Achilles to go unpunished. Achilles was slain when Paris hit him on the heel with a poisoned arrow.

In 'Trapped Dingo' the poet, who feels some responsibility for the death of the she-dingo, becomes Achilles. The mate of the she-dingo is Hector; and the she-dingo, who with great anguish laments the death of her mate, becomes Andromache.

TRAPPED DINGO

So here, twisted in steel, and spoiled with red
your sunlight hide, smelling of death and fear,
they crushed out of your throat the terrible song
you sang in the dark ranges. With what crying
you mourned him! — the drinker of blood, the swift death-bringer
who ran with you many a night; and the night was long.
I heard you, desperate poet. Did you hear
my silent voice take up the cry? — replying:
Achilles is overcome, and Hector dead,
and clay stops many a warrior's mouth, wild singer.

Voice from the hills and the river drunken with rain,
for your lament the long night was too brief.
Hurling your woes at the moon, that old cleaned bone,
till the white shorn mobs of stars on the hill of the sky
huddled and trembled, you tolled him, the rebel one.
Insane Andromache, pacing your towers alone,
death ends the verse you chanted; here you lie.
The lover, the maker of elegies is slain,
and veiled with blood her body's stealthy sun.

JUDITH WRIGHT

Trapped Dingo — A moving poem

(1) The dingo is 'twisted in steel, and spoiled with red'. What has happened to her?

(2) What did the she-dingo do when her mate was killed?

(3) How does the poet feel about the death of the she-dingo?

(4) Why do you think the poet likens the she-dingo to Andromache?

(5) Do you feel sorry for the dead she-dingo? Why?

Being a loser at a dog show is not a very pleasant experience, as Pam Ayres wittily reveals in the following poem.

I'M THE DOG WHO DIDN'T WIN A PRIZE

I'm the dog who didn't win a prize.
I didn't have the Most Appealing Eyes.
All day in this heat, I've been standing on me feet
With dogs of every other shape and size.

I've been harshly disinfected, I've been scrubbed,
I've been festooned in a towel and I've been rubbed;
I've been mercilessly brushed, robbed of all me fleas and dust
And now the judging's over: I've been snubbed!

Was it for obedience I was hailed?
As 'Best Dog in the Show' was I regaled?
O not on your Doggo life, pass me down the carving knife,
I had one thing said about me — it was 'FAILED'.

I never for a moment thought I'd fail.
I thought at least I'd win 'Waggiest Tail'.
But no certificate, rosette or commendation did I get —
Nothing on a kennel door to nail.

I am going in my kennel on my own.
Thank you, no. I do not want a bone.
Do not think you can console me with left-overs in my bowl me
Pride is mortified: I want to be alone.

I've heard it from the worldly and the wise:
'Each dog has his day' they all advise,
But I see to my grief and sorrow, my day must have been tomorrow!
Oh I'm the dog who didn't win a prize!

PAM AYRES

The Dog Who Didn't Win a Prize — Some quick questions

(1)   Who is telling the story? Does this make the poem more successful? Why?

(2)   Do you feel sympathy for the dog in the poem? Give your reasons.

(3)   How does the dog react to its treatment at the dog show?

(4)   'Each dog has his day.' What does this proverb mean? How does the dog in the poem feel about the proverb?

(5)   What does this poem reveal about dog shows?

Cats are lovable creatures, but there are times when they can be very, very annoying.

CATS ON THE ROOF

The street where I board is a forest of flats,
And it's cursed by a plague of most insolent cats.
As soon as the sun has sunk down in the west
They all sally forth on an amorous quest.
A tomcat will call from the top of a roof,
A second will answer from somewhere aloof;
Then others arrive, and the concert begins
As they slither and slide on the tiles and the tins.

Cats on the roof,
Cats on the roof,
Amorous, clamorous
Cats on the roof,
White ones and yellow ones,
Black-as-Othello ones,
Oh, the Devil's in league with the cats on the roof.

They talk of the need for our country's defence,
But it wouldn't involve a great deal of expense
To put on the market some new sort of bombs
To hurl at the tabs and the turbulent toms
Who gather in numbers that nightly increase
To shatter our slumber and slaughter our peace.
An inventor will surely make plenty of oof
Who can deal with the menace of cats on the roof.

They climb and they clamber, they hiss and they wail,
And they go up and down on the musical scale.
A shy young soprano will start on a note
While the ardent old tenor is clearing his throat.
Then off they will go on a dainty duet,
And the bass will come in when the tempo is set;
And any young student of sharps and of flats
Can learn quite a lot from a chorus of cats.

Then all of a sudden the tempo will change —
They really possess a most wonderful range
From alto, contralto, falsetto and bass;
Caruso and Melba are not in the race.
The tenor will rise on a note of his own
And the bass will die off to a horrible moan.
Oh, I doubt if the patience of Job would be proof
'Gainst amorous, clamorous cats on the roof.

A lull may occur when the midnight is past,
And you think you are set for some slumber at last,
But just as you're dozing, your face to the wall,
The concert will end in a general brawl.
And you'll turn on your pillow and mentally vow
To kill every cat that you meet with from now,
Till morning comes in with a dusting of mats,
And another night's rest has been ruined by cats.

Cats on the roof,
Cats on the roof,
Amorous, clamorous
Cats on the roof,
White ones and yellow ones,
Black-as-Othello ones,
Oh, the Devil's in league with the cats on the roof.

EDWARD HARRINGTON

Cats on the Roof — A catalogue of complaints

(1)   What do the cats do to annoy the poet?

(2)   What does the poet mean by 'a forest of flats'?

(3)   When do the cats start making their noise?

(4)   Write down evidence to prove that there are many kinds of cats in the poet's neighbourhood.

(5)   What is one solution the poet suggests for getting rid of the cats? Does he mean it?

(6)   Caruso and Melba were famous opera singers. What is the meaning of 'Caruso and Melba are not in the race'?

(7)   Jot down some of the musical terms the poet uses to describe the sound of the cats.

(8)   The poet could have called his poem 'Cats'. Why is 'Cats on the Roof' a better title?

(9)   Why do you think the poet wrote this poem?

(10)   Did you enjoy the poem? Why or why not?

Poet's Corner

Back round 1930 my old man and I were on a mallee block at Boundary Bend, 50 miles [80 km] down the Murray from Swan Hill. We struck eight droughts and went broke, but I remember the moonlight nights when the willy-wagtails were calling 'Sweet Pretty Creature' to one another. I used to get up and sit by the bank of the big dam and listen to them. Absolute stillness. The dam reflected the mallee trees growing on its banks. Sometimes a pair of emus would come down to the dam to drink. They never drank at the same time. While one was drinking the other would be watching. Then they would stalk away and merge into the moonlight and the mallee scrub.

When we went broke and came to North Melbourne there were no more willy-wagtails to listen to — only cats. They used to keep me awake night after night with their awful howling and brawling. So I wrote 'Cats on the Roof' for the Christmas *Bulletin* of 1934. Then I went droving up in the Kelly country to get away from the cats.

Edward Harrington

The poet A. B. ('Banjo') Paterson provides us with a lively description of the life and habits of a platypus.

OLD MAN PLATYPUS

Far from the trouble and toil of town,
Where the reed-beds sweep and shiver,
Look at a fragment of velvet brown —
Old Man Platypus drifting down,
Drifting along the river.

And he plays and dives in the river bends
In a style that is most elusive;
With few relations and fewer friends,
For Old Man Platypus descends
From a family most exclusive.

He shares his burrow beneath the bank
With his wife and his son and daughter
At the roots of the reeds and the grasses rank;
And the bubbles show where our hero sank
To its entrance under the water.

Safe in their burrow below the falls
They live in a world of wonder,
Where no one visits and no one calls
They sleep like little brown billiard balls
With their beaks tucked neatly under.

And he talks in a deep unfriendly growl
As he goes on his journey lonely;
For he's no relation to fish nor fowl,
Nor to bird nor beast, nor to horned owl,
In fact, he's the one and only!

A. B. PATERSON

Animals — A writing activity

Write an animal poem of your own. Find out as much as you can about its appearance, life and habits. You may like to make it amusing. Read the humorous poems in the Animal Antics section that follows.

Animal Antics

A SHAGGY DOG

There was a small maiden named Maggie,
Whose dog was enormous and shaggy;
The front end of him
Looked vicious and grim —
But the tail end was friendly and waggy.

THE COW

The cow stood on the hillside,
Its skin as smooth as silk;
It slipped upon a cowslip,
And sprained a pint of milk.

CATASTROPHE

There were once two cats of Kilkenny,
Each thought there was one cat too many;
So they fought and they fit,
And they scratched and they bit,
Till, excepting their nails
And the tips of their tails,
Instead of two cats, there weren't any.

WAY DOWN SOUTH

Way down South where bananas grow,
A grasshopper stepped on an elephant's toe;
The elephant said, with tears in his eyes,
'Pick on somebody your own size!'

MY DOG

I've got a dog as thin as a rail,
He's got fleas all over his tail;
Every time his tail goes flop,
The fleas on the bottom all hop to the top.

THE CROCODILE

If you should meet a crocodile,
 Don't take a stick and poke him;
Ignore the welcome in his smile,
 Be careful not to stroke him.
For as he sleeps upon the Nile,
 He thinner gets and thinner;
And whene'er you meet a crocodile
 He's ready for his dinner

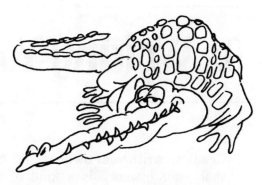

THE TIBETAN ELEPHANT

An elephant born in Tibet,
One day in its cage wouldn't get.
 So its keeper stood near
 Stuck a hose in its ear,
And invented the first Jumbo Jet.

RABBIT

A rabbit raced a turtle,
You know the turtle won;
And Mister Bunny came in late,
A little hot cross bun!

THE BEAR

A cheerful old bear at the Zoo
Could always find something to do.
 When it bored him to go
 On a walk to and fro,
He reversed it and walked fro and to!

THE RHINOCEROS

The rhino is a homely beast,
For human eyes he's not a feast.
Farewell, farewell, you old rhinoceros,
I'll stare at something less prepoceros.

OGDEN NASH

9. Writing Your Own Poems

Ready to write your own poems? A good way to make a start is to imagine that your memory is a kind of reservoir of words and ideas on many different things — each of which is the possible subject of a poem.

A 'Hair' Poem

Look at the words that follow. The first box contains words that describe hair. The second contains words that rhyme with 'hair'.

Descriptive Words				Rhyming Words		
curly	woolly	wavy		bare	tear	care
frizzy	fluffy	crinkly		air	there	wear
wiry	floppy	wispy		rare	flare	glare
tidy	bouncy	shaggy		stare	dare	spare
shiny	skimpy	greasy		fair	share	swear

With these two groups of words you can now begin to think of creating a simple four-line poem by forming the words you choose into a pattern. First the pattern:

1ST LINE: I like hair that is

2ND LINE: ....y, ... y, ...y, ... y.

3RD LINE: ....care.

[your comment, rhyming with 'hair']

4TH LINE: Hair.

Then a poem that follows the pattern:

HAIR

I like hair that is
Healthy, wavy, shiny, tidy.
I brush mine with care,
Hair.

Next, write a 'Hair' poem of your own. But before you do, read through 'Spaghetti' (below), so that you become thoroughly acquainted with the pattern.

SPAGHETTI

I like spaghetti that is
Lengthy, loopy, wormy, slithery.
Superbly prepared by Lucetti,
Spaghetti.

Now, given a different subject — Ants — try fitting your own words into the same pattern. Don't forget to turn on the tap to your personal mental reservoir of words and ideas about this busy topic.

I like ants that are
.............y, ...y, ...y, ...y.
....,
Ants.

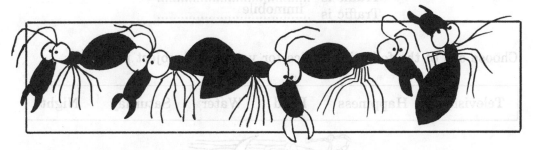

And here are some more 'I like' topics to pattern into your own poems:

| Dogs | Cheese | Fish | Toes | Trees | Tea | Eggs | School |

Love and Hate

Let's look at a different poem-pattern — a simple but effective two-line form based on love and hate. Here's the pattern:

I love ....
I hate ....

EXAMPLES:

I love ...apples...............
I hate ...worms...............

I love ...television............
I hate ...commercials.........

Note the special link between the thing loved and the thing hated. Remember, as you write your own love/hate poems, to try for such a link. This will add the necessary zip to your twin lines. After all, most good things do have a bad side too.

Subject Poems

A poem you could try is one in which the subject remains the same while you supply a series of fitting descriptive words. It goes as follows:

Traffic is ...thick...........................
Traffic is ...fast............................
Traffic is ...noisy...........................
Traffic is ...dangerous....................
Traffic is ...obnoxious.....................
Traffic is ...carbon monoxide............
Traffic is ...bumper to bumper..........
Traffic is ...immobile......................

Choose one of the following topics for your own 'subject poem':

Television	Happiness	Food	Water	Saturday	Night

Three-Word Poems

Three words starting with the same letter — a noun, a verb and an adverb (usually a *-ly* word) — provide the pattern for another satisfying style of poem. For example:

Bees	(noun)
Buzz	(verb)
Busily	(adverb)

Note the vertical arrangement, and the fact that all three words begin with a 'B'. Try completing the following:

Teachers	Gulls	A................s
Talk	G...............	Amble
T...............	Gracefully	Aimlessly

Alphabet Poems

The following poem is as simple as ABC. In fact, it *is* an alphabet poem. Each line consists of a noun (the subject) followed by a verb and an adverb. You are given the noun plus either the verb or the adverb. All you have to do to complete the poem is to think up a fitting or appropriate word to fill the gap in each line. See how you go. (Note that the first line is done for you as an example.)

ALPHABET POEM

Apes	ACT	AMUSINGLY
Baboons	BABBLE	....
Cows	....	CONTENTEDLY
Dachshunds	DIG	....
Elephants	....	ERRATICALLY
Flies	FLIT	....
Goats	....	GREEDILY
Hyenas	HOWL	....
Insects	....	INTENSELY
Jumbucks	JUMP	....
Kangaroos	....	KNOWINGLY
Lions	LEAP	....
Monkeys	....	MISCHIEVOUSLY
Nitwits	NAG	....
Octopuses	....	OBNOXIOUSLY

Panthers	POUNCE	....
Quadrupeds	....	QUICKLY
Rattlesnakes	RATTLE	....
Skunks	....	SHOCKINGLY
Toads	TRAVEL	....
Unicorns	....	USELESSLY
Vampires	VISIT	....
Whales	....	WONDERFULLY
Yaks	YABBER	....
Zombies	....	ZESTFULLY

Writing Couplets

A *couplet* is a couple or pair of lines of verse that go together. A famous couplet that stands all by itself as a poem is this one by the poet Ezra Pound:

IN A STATION OF THE METRO

> The apparition of these faces in the crowd;
> Petals on a wet, black bough.

EZRA POUND

In this kind of couplet the second line stems from, or is suggested by, the first line. Pound's first line brings out the strange and ghostly appearance (apparition) of the pale faces of a crowd of people as they emerge from the dark and grimy exit of a subway station. Such faces suggest to the poet the image of flower-petals ranged against the dark, wet bough (branch) of a tree.

Let's look at some more examples of couplets:

A honey-bee frantically filling her pollen sacs in a flower;
Shoppers feverishly stuffing their string bags at a sale.

> Jet trails in the empty sky;
> On the blackboard chalk-scrawls fly.

Ants pouring out of their nest;
Schoolchildren emptying out into the playground.

> A powerful truck roaring up the highway;
> A lion bounding towards its prey.

Grey smoke spiralling up from a logfire;
A ghost floating up a staircase.

Using a Poem as a Model

Carefully read through the poem 'Giraffes'. Then, using the 'Because...'
idea, write a poem of your own on another topic.

GIRAFFES

I like them.
Ask me why.
Because they hold their heads so high.
Because their necks stretch to the sky.
Because they're quiet, calm, and shy.
Because they run so fast they fly.
Because their eyes are velvet brown.
Because their coats are spotted tan.
Because they eat the tops of trees.
Because their legs have knobbly knees.
Because
Because
Because. That's why
I like giraffes.

MARY ANN HOBERMAN

Haiku

These subtle three-line Japanese poems are a delight to read. Study the
haiku that follow and then try writing some of your own. What you need
to remember is that the first line should have five syllables, the second line
seven syllables, and the last line five syllables — seventeen syllables in all.

The following selection contains traditional Japanese haiku, as well as
two newer ones.

Going yesterday,
Today, tonight ... the wild geese
Have all gone, honking.

TANIGUCHI BUSON (1716–1783)

Snow having melted,
The whole village is brimful
Of happy children.

ISSA (1763–1827)

You summer grasses!
Glorious dreams of great warriors
Now only ruins.

MATSUO BASHŌ (1644–1694)

The servant's day off.
Does he dream of that as on
The stove red beans boil?

TANIGUCHI BUSON

A wayside sermon
All nonsense to me, but see
How serene he is!

ISSA

You rice-field maidens!
The only things not muddy
Are the songs you sing.

RAIZAN (1654–1716)

Gold chrysanthemums!
White chrysanthemums! Others
Need not be mentioned.

RANSETSU (1654–1707)

Both plains and mountains
Have been captured by the snow —
There is nothing left.

JŌSŌ (1662–1704)

With your fists ablaze
with letters and coloured stamps
beautiful mailman.

PAUL GOODMAN

Orange and golden
the *New York Times* is blazing
in the village dump.

PAUL GOODMAN

10. Humorous Poems

One poet's opinion of the character and habits of the shark is expressed in the poem that follows. Note that the first half of the poem — down to 'asleep' — is about the shark's pretended lack of interest in you, his prey, as you undress on the beach. But as soon as you leap into the sea and get within the shark's range, his true character comes out. Then, it's 'no use crying or appealing'. Why not?

As well as warning you about the shark, what does the poem urge you to do? What is the poet's final judgment about the nature of the shark?

THE SHARK

A treacherous monster is the Shark,
He never makes the least remark.

And when he sees you on the sand,
He doesn't seem to want to land.

He watches you take off your clothes,
And not the least excitement shows.

His eyes do not grow bright or roll,
He has astounding self-control.

He waits till you are quite undrest,
And seems to take no interest.

And when towards the sea you leap,
He looks as if he were asleep.

But when you once get in his range,
His whole demeanour seems to change.

He throws his body right about,
And his true character comes out.

It's no use crying or appealing,
He seems to lose all decent feeling.

After this warning you will wish
To keep clear of this treacherous fish.

His back is black, his stomach white,
He has a very dangerous bite.

LORD ALFRED DOUGLAS

THE WASP HE IS A NASTY ONE

The wasp he is a nasty one
He scavenges and thrives,
Unlike the honest honey bee
He doesn't care for hives.
He builds his waxy nest
Then brings his mates from near and far
To sneak into your house
When you have left the door ajar.

Then sniffing round for jam he goes,
In every pot and packet,
Buzzing round the kitchen
In his black and yellow jacket.
If with a rolled-up paper
He should spot you creeping near
He will do a backward somersault
And sting you on the ear!

You never know with wasps,
You can't relax, not for a minute
Whatever you pick up — Look out!
A wasp might still be in it.
You never even know
If there's a wasp against your chest,
For wasps are very fond
Of getting folded in your vest.

And he *always* comes in summer.
In the winter-time he's gone
When you never go on picnics
And you've put a jersey on.
I mean, what other single comment
Causes panic and despair
Like someone saying, 'Keep still!
There's a wasp caught in your hair!'

But in a speeding car
He finds his favourite abode,
He likes poor Dad to swat like mad
And veer across the road.
He likes to watch Dad's face,
As all the kids begin to shout,
'Dad! I don't like wasps!
Oh where's he gone, Dad? Get him *out!*'

And I'd like to make a reference
To all the men who say,
'Don't antagonize it
And the wasp will go away,'
For I've done a little survey
To see if it will or won't,
And they sting you if you hit them
And they sting you if you don't.

As we step into the sunshine
Through the summers and the springs,
Carrying our cardigans
And nursing all our stings,
I often wonder, reaching for the blue bag
Just once more,
If all things have a purpose
What on earth can *wasps* be for?

PAM AYRES

The Wasp — Some stinging questions

(1) According to the poet, how does the nature of the wasp differ from
that of the honey bee?

(2)   'In every pot and packet, / Buzzing round the kitchen . . . .' What is the wasp looking for?

(3)   How does Pam Ayres describe the colouring of the wasp?

(4)   What would be the purpose of the 'rolled-up paper' mentioned in the second stanza?

(5)   Why can you not relax even for a moment when wasps are around?

(6)   What part of your anatomy is in particular danger from the wasp?

(7)   In what season of the year does the wasp *always* arrive?

(8)   What kind of trouble does the wasp like to cause in a speeding car?

(9)   Pam Ayres has done a little survey on wasps to see whether they will really go away if you don't antagonize them. What is her conclusion?

(10)   What does Pam Ayres wonder about wasps in the last stanza?

Have you ever had an item of clothing that you couldn't give up, though it threatened to fall to pieces on you? If so, you'll feel particularly sympathetic towards the wearer of the shirt in the next poem. And who knows — you might even save the pieces as they fall off you, and keep them somewhere special. . . .

I'VE HAD THIS SHIRT

I've had this shirt
that's covered in dirt
for years and years and years.

It used to be red
but I wore it in bed
and it went grey
cos I wore it all day
for years and years and years.

The arms fell off
in the Monday wash
and you can see my vest
through the holes in the chest
for years and years and years.

As my shirt falls apart
I'll keep the bits
in a biscuit tin
on the mantelpiece
for years and years and years.

MICHAEL ROSEN

The poor customer in the following poem finds an alligator swimming around in his coffee. But, as if this weren't enough, he fails to get even a scrap of sympathy or co-operation in his efforts to rid his beverage of its unwelcome foreign body.

WAITER! . . . THERE'S AN ALLIGATOR IN MY COFFEE

Waiter! . . . there's an alligator in my coffee.
Are you trying to be funny?
he said:
what do you want for a dime . . .?
. . . a circus?
but sir! I said,
he's swimming
around
and around
in my coffee
and he might
jump out on the table . . .
Feed him a lump of sugar! he snarled —
no! . . . make it two;
it'll weigh him down
and he'll drown.

I dropped two blocks of sugar
into the swamp,
two grist jaws snapped them up
and the critter —
he never drowned.
Waiter! . . . there's an alligator in my coffee.
Kill him! Kill him!
he said:
BASH HIS BRAINS OUT
WITH YOUR SPOON . . . !
By this time
considerable attention had been drawn:
around my coffee
the waiters, the owner,
and customers gathered.

What seems to be the trouble?
the owner inquired,
and I replied:
There's an alligator in my coffee!
. . . But the coffee's fresh, he said
and raised the cup to his nose . . .
Careful! I said,
he'll bite it
off
and he replied:
How absurd,
and lowered the cup
level to his mouth and
swallowed
the evidence.

JOE ROSENBLATT

Alligator Coffee — Some snappy questions

(1)   What smart retort does the waiter make in response to the customer's complaint?

(2)   What does the customer fear?

(3)   Why does the waiter suggest that the customer feed the alligator two lumps of sugar?

(4)   What happens to the sugar-cubes when the customer drops them into the coffee?

(5)   What point does the owner make about the coffee?

(6)   Why is the alligator referred to as 'evidence'?

Archy and Mehitabel are two creations of the poet Don Marquis. Archy is a cockroach and Mehitabel is a cat. Archy, in particular, is very talented and writes poetry by throwing himself on the keys of a typewriter — although he can't manage capitals or punctuation marks, which are therefore absent from Archy's poems. Here's how Don Marquis describes his strange discovery of Archy at work:

> We came into our room earlier than usual in the morning, and discovered a gigantic cockroach jumping about upon the keys.
>
> He did not see us, and we watched him. He would climb painfully upon the framework of the machine and cast himself with all his force upon a key, head downward, and his weight and the impact of the blow were just sufficient to operate the machine, one slow letter after another. He could not work the capital letters, and he had a great deal of difficulty operating the mechanism that shifts the paper so that a fresh line may be started. We never saw a cockroach work so hard or perspire so freely in all our lives before. After about an hour of this frightfully difficult literary labour he fell to the floor exhausted, and we saw him creep feebly into a nest of the poems which are always there in profusion.

Now for a poem by Archy himself. Notice, as you read, just *how* Archy reviews the book that forms the subject of the poem.

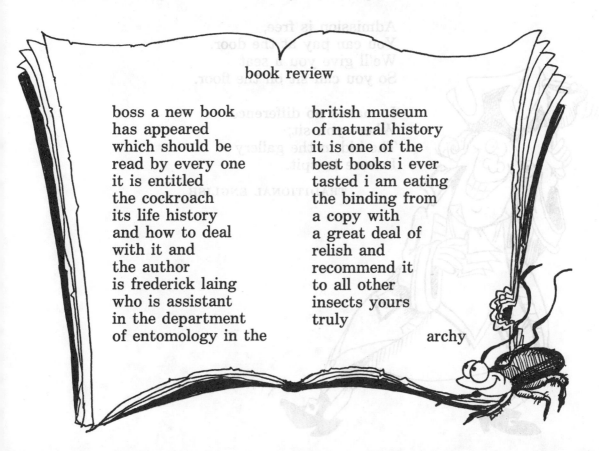

book review

boss a new book
has appeared
which should be
read by every one
it is entitled
the cockroach
its life history
and how to deal
with it and
the author
is frederick laing
who is assistant
in the department
of entomology in the
british museum
of natural history
it is one of the
best books i ever
tasted i am eating
the binding from
a copy with
a great deal of
relish and
recommend it
to all other
insects yours
truly

archy

If you have a twisted sense of humour, or feel you would *like* to have one, read this poem.

LADLES AND JELLYSPOONS

Ladles and jellyspoons:
I come before you
To stand behind you
And tell you something
I know nothing about.

Next Thursday,
The day after Friday,
There'll be a ladies' meeting
For men only.

Wear your best clothes
If you haven't any,
And if you can come
Please stay home.

Admission is free,
You can pay at the door.
We'll give you a seat
So you can sit on the floor.

It makes no difference
Where you sit;
The kid in the gallery
Is sure to spit.

TRADITIONAL ENGLISH

Pam Ayres takes a sharp look at some unruly little visitors.

PLEASE WILL YOU TAKE YOUR CHILDREN HOME
BEFORE I DO THEM IN

Please will you take your children home
Before I do them in?
I kissed your little son
As he came posturing within.
I took his little jacket
And removed his little hat
But now the visit's over
So push off you little brat.

And don't think for a moment
That I didn't understand
How the hatchet he was waving
In his grotty little hand
Broke my china teapot
That I've always held so dear —
But would you mind removing him
Before I smack his ear?

Of course I wasn't angry
As I shovelled up the dregs,
I'm only glad the teabags
Didn't scald his little legs.
I'm glad he liked my chocolate cake,
I couldn't help but laugh
As he rubbed it in the carpet . . .
Would he like the other half?

He guzzled all the orange
And he guzzled all the Coke —
The only thing that kept me sane
Was hoping he might choke.
And then he had a mishap,
Well, I couldn't bear to look,
Do something for your Auntie little sunshine . . .
Sling your hook.

He's been playing in the garden
And he's throttled all the flowers,
Give the lad a marlinspike
He'll sit out there for hours.
I've gathered my insecticides
And marked them with their name
And put them up where children
Couldn't reach them. That's a shame.

Still he must have liked my dog
Because he choked her half to death,
She'll go out for another game
Once she's caught her breath.
He rode her round the garden
And he lashed her with his rope,
She's never bitten anyone
But still, we live in hope.

He's kicked the TV now!
I like to see it getting booted,
Kick it one more time son
You might get electrocuted!
Yes, turn up the volume,
Twist the knobs, me little treasure
And when the programme's over
There's the door. It's been a pleasure.

PAM AYRES

Before I Do Them In — Twelve little questions

(1) 'I kissed your little son', Pam Ayres tells his parent(s). But what does she call the 'little son' further on in the stanza?

(2) How did Pam's china teapot get broken?

(3) What does she threaten to do to the boy if he is not removed?

(4) In the course of the third stanza, Pam Ayres waxes sarcastic. Explain how she does this.

(5) What kept the poet sane when the boy guzzled all the orange and all the Coke?

(6) 'And then he had a mishap....' What do you think happened?

(7) What do you think the expression 'Sling your hook' means?

(8) In what kind of playing has the boy been engaged in the garden?

(9)   In what three ways did the boy make the poet's dog suffer?

(10)   'But still, we live in hope.' In hope of what?

(11)   Why did Pam Ayres 'like to see' the boy booting the TV?

(12)   What will happen to the boy when the TV programme finishes?

Mr and Mrs Kartoffel are a very eccentric couple, as you are about to find out.

MR KARTOFFEL

Mr Kartoffel's a whimsical man;
He drinks his beer from a watering can,
And for no good reason that I can see
He fills his pockets with china tea.
He parts his hair with a knife and fork
And takes his ducks for a Sunday walk.
Says he, 'If my wife and I should choose
To wear our stockings outside our shoes,
Plant tulip bulbs in the baby's pram
And eat tobacco instead of jam
And fill the bath with cauliflowers,
That's nobody's business at all but ours.'
Says Mrs K, 'I may choose to travel
With a sack of grass or a sack of gravel,
Or paint my toes, one black, one white,
Or sit on a bird's nest half the night —
But whatever I do that is rum or rare,
I rather think that it's my affair.
So fill up your pockets with stamps and string,
And let us be ready for anything!'
Says Mr K to his whimsical wife,
'How can we face the storms of life,
Unless we are ready for anything?
So if you've provided the stamps and string,
Let us pump up the saddle and harness the horse
And fill him with carrots and custard and sauce,
Let us leap on him lightly and give him a shove
And it's over the sea and away, my love!'

JAMES REEVES

Mr Kartoffel — Match up the eccentricities

See if you can match up the actions on the left with their eccentric completions on the right. Note the example.

He drinks his beer	in the baby's pram.
He fills his pockets	with a sack of grass or gravel.
He parts his hair	from a watering can.
They wear their stockings	one black, one white.
They plant tulip bulbs	with cauliflowers.
They eat tobacco	half the night.
They fill the bath	with carrots, custard and sauce.
She may choose to travel	and harness the horse.
She may paint her toes	instead of jam.
She may sit on a bird's nest	with china tea.
Let us pump up the saddle	outside their shoes.
Let us fill up the horse	with a knife and fork.

The redback spider can be a nasty creature at the best of times. But when he attacks you on the toilet seat — well, that's *really* hitting below the belt!

THE REDBACK ON THE TOILET SEAT

There was a redback on the toilet seat
When I was there last night.
I didn't see him in the dark,
But boy I felt his bite.

I jumped high up into the air
And when I hit the ground,
That crafty redback spider
Wasn't nowhere to be found.

I rushed in to the Missus,
Told her just where I'd been bit.
She grabbed a cut-throat razor-blade
And I nearly took a fit.

I said, 'Just forget what's on your mind
And call a doctor please,

Cause I got a feeling that your cure
Is worse than the disease.'

There was a redback on the toilet seat
When I was there last night.
I didn't see him in the dark,
But boy I felt his bite.

And now I'm here in hospital
A sad and sorry sight,
And I curse the redback spider
On the toilet seat last night.

I can't lie down, I can't sit up
And I don't know what to do,
And all the nurses think it's funny
But that's not my point of view.

I tell you it's embarrassing,
And that's to say the least,
That I'm too sick to eat a bite
While that spider had a feast.

And when I get back home again
I tell you what I'll do,
I'll make that redback suffer
For the pain I'm going through.

I've had so many needles
That I'm looking like a sieve,
And I promise you that spider
Hasn't very long to live.

There was a redback on the toilet seat
When I was there last night.
I didn't see him in the dark,
But boy I felt his bite.

But now I'm here in hospital
A sad and sorry sight,
And I curse the redback spider
On the toilet seat last night.

SLIM NEWTON

The Redback — Unjumble the disaster

Things happen and thoughts occur in a definite order, from the poet's being bitten to his arrival in hospital. Here are the things and the thoughts — but jumbled up. See if you can put them back into their correct order.

- the Missus grabs a razor
- he curses the redback spider
- he's too sick to eat
- he's bitten by the redback in the dark
- he can't lie down and he can't sit up
- the nurses think it's funny
- he jumps high into the air
- embarrassment!
- he's like a sieve because of all the needles
- he threatens to make that redback suffer
- he's a sad and sorry sight in hospital
- he rushes in to the Missus

Creepy-Crawlies and Friends

TODAY I SAW A LITTLE WORM

Today I saw a little worm
Wriggling on his belly.
Perhaps he'd like to come inside
And see what's on the Telly.

SPIKE MILLIGAN

FLIGHTY FLEAS

An odd little thing is a flea
You can't tell a he from a she
But he can, and she can —
Whoopee!

LONGING

I wish I was a little grub
With whiskers round my tummy
I'd climb into a honey-pot
And make my tummy gummy.

HELLO MR PYTHON

Hello Mr Python
Curling round a tree,
Bet you'd like to make yourself
A dinner out of me.

Can't you change your habits
Crushing people's bones?
I wouldn't like a dinner
That emitted fearful groans.

SPIKE MILLIGAN

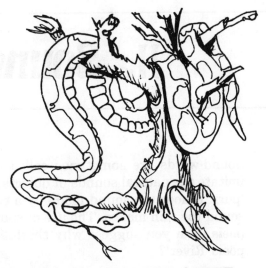

A CENTIPEDE WAS HAPPY QUITE

A centipede was happy quite,
    Until a frog in fun
Said, 'Pray, which leg comes after which?'
This raised her mind to such a pitch,
She lay distracted in the ditch
    Considering how to run.

THE TINY ANT

Said a tiny Ant
To the Elephant
'Mind how you tread in this clearing!'

But alas! Cruel fate!
She was crushed by the weight
Of an elephant, hard of hearing.

SPIKE MILLIGAN

11. Sound-Words

Sound-words are sometimes called *echoic* words because they echo and imitate the natural sounds of objects, things, people and actions. The word 'purr' echoes the sound made by a cat, just as 'pitter-patter' imitates the sound the rain makes. The use of sound-words in poetry is called **onomatopoeia**. Can you suggest why the following poem is called 'The Onomatopoeia River'?

THE ONOMATOPOEIA RIVER

Glade ... shade ... pool ... cool ...
Fickle trickle ... supple ... able ...
Yearning ... trending ... wending.

(Read each line faster.)
Amble, addle, dawdle, dabble,
babble, bubble, gurgle, gambol,
bustle hustle tussle tumble,
mumble-grumble-rumble, hurtle-
Lunge! Plunge!
Splash! Spray,
flay, fume.
Gnash! Lash! Rage, wage.

(Read each line slower.)
Freed, speed ...
weed ... reed ...
haze ... laze ...
hide ... glide ...
wide ... tide.

MAX DUNN

What sound-words has the cartoonist of 'Footrot Flats' used in this comic strip?

Making Up Sound-Words

Some poets, such as Stephen Hewitt and Philip Paddon, have gone so far as to create their own sound-words — and what a wonderful job they have done of it in 'In the Bath' and 'Muddy Boots'. See whether you can find at least eight home-made sound-words in each of these two poems.

IN THE BATH

I schlunch into the bath
Then I gollop, and schollop and drollop
The water on the walls,
I slop and I querch as the soap is
Speeding around the bottom of the
Bath.
Then I stand up and hulunch
Back into the water.
I flunch and I smollop the water
Around till I whallop, and smack the
Water out.

STEPHEN HEWITT

MUDDY BOOTS

Trudging down the country lane,
Splodgely thlodgely plooph,
Two foot deep in slimy mud.
Faloomph Polopf Gallooph.
Hopolosplodgely go your boots,
Slopthopy gruthalamie golumph.
Then you find firm ground again,
Plonky shlonky clonky.
BUT ... then you sink back in again,
Squelchy crathpally hodgle.

Sitting outside scraping your boots,
Sclapey gulapy criketty,
Cursing the horrible six inch slodge,
Scrapey flakey cakey.
Flakes of mud, crispling off the boots,
Crinkey splinky schlinkle.
Never again, will I venture into that
... Schlodgely, Flopchely, Thlodgely,
schrinkshely, slimy, grimy, squelchy, ghastly MUD!

PHILIP PADDON

Here's a tense game of ping-pong, full of sound and fury.

PING-PONG

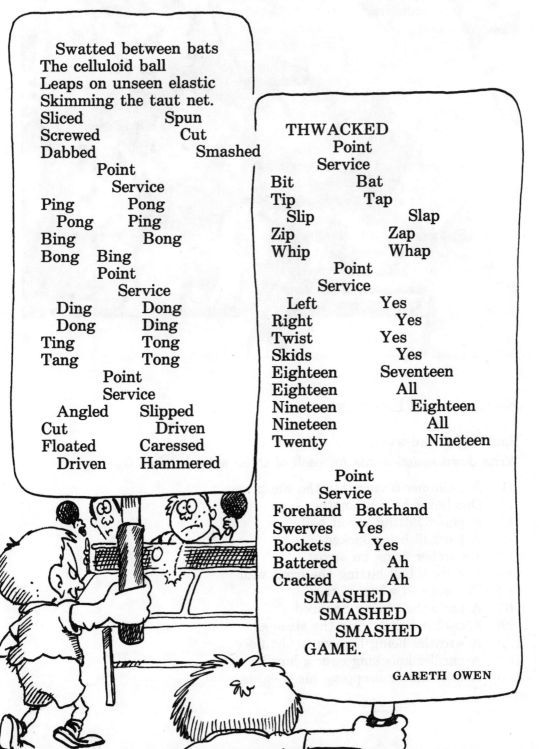

Swatted between bats
The celluloid ball
Leaps on unseen elastic
Skimming the taut net.
Sliced   Spun
Screwed   Cut
Dabbed   Smashed
          Point
               Service
Ping   Pong
  Pong   Ping
Bing   Bong
Bong   Bing
          Point
               Service
Ding   Dong
Dong   Ding
Ting   Tong
Tang   Tong
          Point
               Service
  Angled   Slipped
Cut   Driven
Floated   Caressed
  Driven   Hammered

THWACKED
     Point
     Service
Bit   Bat
Tip   Tap
  Slip   Slap
Zip   Zap
Whip   Whap
          Point
     Service
  Left   Yes
Right   Yes
Twist   Yes
Skids   Yes
Eighteen   Seventeen
Eighteen   All
Nineteen   Eighteen
Nineteen   All
Twenty   Nineteen

     Point
     Service
Forehand   Backhand
Swerves   Yes
Rockets   Yes
Battered   Ah
Cracked   Ah
  SMASHED
     SMASHED
          SMASHED
GAME.

GARETH OWEN

Some Sound Exercises

Sporting sound-words

Write down sound-words for each of these actions taken from sport.

(1) A swimmer diving into the water
(2) One boxer hitting another
(3) A golfer hitting a golf ball
(4) A football being kicked
(5) An archer firing an arrow
(6) A squash ball hitting the front wall
(7) The start of a motor race
(8) A basketball being bounced
(9) A cricket ball hitting the stumps
(10) A wrestler being thrown to the floor
(11) A hurdler knocking over a hurdle
(12) A weightlifter dropping his weights

Sound-words in action

Here are some sound-words. Write down what or who you think was responsible for each of them (e.g. *crash* — plates falling from a table onto the floor). You'll find that there are quite a few possibilities for each answer. Good fun can be had if every member of the class reads out some answers.

thud	bang	splatter	splash	fizz	drip
mumble	tinkle	clang	rattle	squelch	rumble
thump	chirp	shuffle	crunch	slash	screech
bong	flip	chatter	boom	flutter	throb
hiss	murmur	whizz	slam	slurp	twang
sizzle	crackle	whallop	slither	ooze	clatter
plop	bump	giggle	pop	ping	gurgle

Sound-words and Garfield

Read through the 'Garfield' cartoon, then write down the sound-words. When you have done this, write down the action or occurrence each of the sound-words is representing.

12. Around the Neighbourhood

You can't help but like Luigi. He eats a lot, sings a bit, but above all he's the poet's best friend.

MY FRIEND LUIGI

My friend Luigi keeps
  A delicatessen store
And all along the counters are
  Delicious foods galore
Like roll-mops, Russian salad,
  Liver pâté and cole-slaw!

My friend Luigi is
  As fat as a Dutch cheese,
It must be years and years and years
  Since he last saw his knees.
Well, what on earth can you expect
  Among such treats as these?

My friend Luigi likes
  To nibble all day long,
And sometimes when he's feeling gay
  He warbles into song
Although he cannot sing in tune
  And all the notes are wrong.

But my friend Luigi though
  He's short and fat and dressed
In tight green stripey trousers
  And a red and white striped vest
Of all my friends Luigi is
  The one I love the best.

JOHN SMITH

There are times when being a 'housewife' is the most difficult occupation in the world.

THE HOUSEWIFE'S LAMENT

The Yorkshire pud is burning
I don't know what to do.
The cabbage water's boiling
I wouldn't have a clue.
The goddam kids are screaming
My eardrums are dead.
A thumping migraine's coming
I'm going off my head.
My nails are getting shorter
That nasty habit's back.
The kids are screaming louder
The dog's chewed up my mac.
The telly's on full tilt
My head's begun to spin
The kids are grinning, full of guilt
I'm going to have a gin.
The cat has ruined the carpet
The old man's just come in
The twins smashed the radio set
This mess is just a sin.
Dad shouts, 'Cup of tea, dear'
The dog barks at the door
There's plenty of noise to hear
But I can take no more.
'Get it yourself, you parasite
And all you kids shut up!'
And how I screamed with all my might
It's early to bed tonight.

ALAN WELLS

The Housewife's Lament — When everything goes wrong

Re-examine 'The Housewife's Lament' and explain what goes wrong with each of the following. (The exercise continues overleaf.)

The Yorkshire pud	
The cabbage water	

The kids	
The cat	
The dog	
The housewife's head	
Her nails	
Her eardrums	
The television	
The radio	
Dad	

The smells, sights and sounds of the fish shop never fail to delight us.

FISH AND CHIPS

Fish and chips today for tea,
A fish for Gran, a fish for me.
I buy them at the corner place,
From smiling Meg of rosy face.

Meg sees the small boys lick their lips
At battered fish and golden chips.
Her apron's white, her hands are red;
She sees the hungry thousands fed.

For sixpence more there're peas as well,
Mushy peas with gorgeous smell;
And butter beans on Friday night,
Pale, steaming beans for your delight.

The counter's white, the walls are pink,
The shelves hold lemonade to drink.
The fat is hissing in the pan,
And soon I hurry home to Gran.

The chips look good; they taste the same;
They've won our Meg some local fame.
Fish and chips today for tea,
A fish for Gran, a fish for me.

A. ELLIOTT-CANNON

Fish and Chips — Fishing for clues

(1) What clue suggests that Meg enjoys her work?

(2) What clues indicate that Meg works hard?

(3) What clue reveals that small boys love Meg's fish and chips?

(4) What clue suggests that the poet loves Meg's peas?

(5) What clues suggest that the child loves Gran?

(6) What clue indicates that the child is looking forward to eating the fish and chips on arriving at home?

(7) What clue shows that Meg does not sell only food?

(8) What clues suggest that these childhood experiences in Meg's shop have made an unforgettable impression on the poet?

LATE NIGHT WALK DOWN TERRY STREET

A policeman on a low-powered motorcycle stops.
His radio crackles, his helmet yellows.

Empty buses heading for the depot
Rush past the open end of Terry Street.

In their light, a man with a bike walking home,
Too drunk to ride it, turns into Terry Street.

Taxis swerve down Terry Street's shortcut,
Down uneven halls of Street Lighting Department Yellow,

Into which now comes the man with the bike,
Struggling to keep on his legs.

The policeman waits under a gone-out streetlamp.
He stops the drunk, they talk, they laugh together.

I pass them then, beside dark, quiet houses,
In others mumbling sounds of entertainment;

Cathode-glows through curtains, faint latest tunes;
Creaking of bedsprings, lights going out.

DOUGLAS DUNN

Down Terry Street — An eventful walk

What are some of the things the poet sees and hears as he takes a night walk down Terry Street? Answer this question using the list below.

Sights and Sounds of Terry Street

Policeman	
Man with a bike	
Houses	
Vehicles	

Life on the move can present all kinds of problems for a family.

DRIFTERS

One day soon he'll tell her it's time to start packing,
and the kids will yell 'Truly?' and get wildly excited for no reason,
and the brown kelpie pup will start dashing about, tripping everyone up,
and she'll go out to the vegetable-patch and pick up all the green tomatoes from the vines,
and notice how the oldest girl is close to tears because she was happy here,
and how the youngest girl is beaming because she wasn't.
And the first thing she'll put on the trailer will be the bottling-set she never unpacked from Grovedale,
and when the loaded ute bumps down the drive past the blackberry-canes with their last shrivelled fruit,
she won't even ask why they're leaving this time, or where they're heading for
— she'll only remember how, when they came here,
she held out her hands bright with berries,
the first of the season, and said:
'Make a wish, Tom, make a wish.'

BRUCE DAWE

Drifters — Looking at a family on the move

(1) Why is the poem entitled 'Drifters'?

(2) Why will the dog start 'dashing about' and 'tripping everyone up'?

(3) How will the oldest girl react to the decision to move? Why?

(4) Why will Tom's wife not have unpacked the bottling-set?

(5) She 'won't even ask why they're leaving this time'. Why do you think she will adopt this attitude?

(6) On their arrival at the house they will soon be leaving, 'she held out her hands bright with berries'. How did the berries signify hope for the family?

(7) By the time of the family's departure, the berries will have become 'shrivelled fruit'. How does the change in the berries also relate to the drifters themselves?

(8) Do you feel sorry for Tom's wife? Why or why not?

'Corner' is a poem about a tense battle of wits between a policeman and the poet, who describes the incident at first hand.

CORNER

The cop slumps alertly on his motorcycle,
Supported by one leg like a leather stork.
His glance accuses me of loitering.
I can see his eyes moving like a fish
In the green depths of his green goggles.

His ease is fake. I can tell.
My ease is fake. And he can tell.
The fingers armored by his gloves
Splay and clench, itching to change something.
As if he were my enemy or my death,
I just standing there watching.

I spit out my gum which has gone stale.
I knock out a new cigarette —
Which is my bravery.
It is all imperceptible:
The way I shift my weight,
The way he creaks in his saddle.

The traffic is specific though constant.
The sun surrounds me, divides the street between us.
His crash helmet is whiter in the shade.
It is like a bull ring as they say it is just before the fighting.
I cannot back down. I am there.

Everything holds me back.
I am in danger of disappearing into the sunny dust.
My levis bake and my T shirt sweats.

My cigarette makes my eyes burn.
But I don't dare drop it.

Who made him my enemy?
Prince of coolness. King of fear.
Why do I lean here waiting?
Why does he lounge there watching?

I am becoming sunlight.
My hair is on fire. My boots run like tar.
I am hung-up by the bright air.

Something breaks through all of a sudden,
And he blasts off, quick as a craver,
Smug in his power; watching me watch.

RALPH POMEROY

Corner — Understanding

(1)   Why does the policeman look like 'a leather stork'?

(2)   What are the policeman's eyes compared to?

(3)   What words in the poem convey the feeling of heat?

(4)   Why does the poet consider the policeman 'Prince of coolness' and 'King of fear'?

(5)   How is the cigarette a part of the poet's bravery?

(6)   'But I don't dare drop it.' Why does the poet not dare to drop his cigarette?

(7)   Why do you think Pomeroy has called the poem 'Corner'?

(8)   'I cannot back down.' Why is this? What battle of wits is going on between the policeman and the poet?

Issues for Discussion

(1) What is your attitude to the police?
(2) Why is a police force important in our society?
(3) Do you think police sometimes unnecessarily antagonize young people?
(4) Do young people sometimes unnecessarily provoke the police?

A girl is alone and cold as she suffers 'the first frost of having been hurt'.

FIRST FROST

A girl is freezing in a telephone booth,
huddled in her flimsy coat,
her face stained by tears
and smeared with lipstick.

She breathes on her thin little fingers.
Fingers like ice. Glass beads in her ears.

She has to beat her way back alone
down the icy street.

First frost. A beginning of losses.
The first frost of telephone phrases.

It is the start of winter glittering on her cheek,
the first frost of having been hurt.

ANDREI VOZNESENSKY

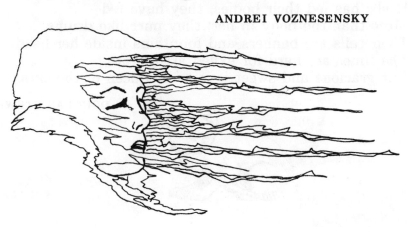

That it is better to give than to receive is seen clearly in 'Lady Feeding the Cats'.

LADY FEEDING THE CATS

Shuffling along in her broken shoes from the slums,
A blue-eyed lady showing the weather's stain,
Her long dress green and black like a pine in the rain,
Her bonnet much bedraggled, daily she comes
Uphill past the Moreton Bays and the smoky gums
With a sack of bones on her back and a song in her brain
To feed those outlaws prowling about the Domain,
Those furtive she-cats and those villainous toms.

Proudly they step to meet her, they march together
With an arching of backs and a waving of plumy tails
And smiles that swear they never would harm a feather.
They rub at her legs for the bounty that never fails,
They think she is a princess out of a tower,
And so she is, she is trembling with love and power.

Meat, it is true, is meat, and demands attention,
But this is the sweetest moment that they know
Whose courtship even is a hiss, a howl and a blow.
And so much kindness passing their comprehension
— Beggars and rogues who never deserved this pension —
Some recollection of old punctilio
Dawns in their eyes, and as she moves to go
They turn their battered heads in condescension.

She smiles and walks back lightly to the slums.
If she has fed their bodies, they have fed
More than the body in her; they purr like drums,
Their tails are banners and fountains inside her head.
The times are hard for exiled aristocrats,
But gracious and sweet it is to be queen of the cats.

DOUGLAS STEWART

Lady Feeding the Cats — Reading closely

(1) What does the word 'shuffling' suggest about the lady?

(2) What words suggest that the lady is poor?

(3) Why do you think the poet refers to the cats as outlaws? What other words continue this idea?

(4) The lady is seen as 'trembling with love and power'. What power does she have over the cats?

(5) Jot down the words that represent the sounds made by the cats.

(6) How does the lady feel after she has fed the cats? Why?

(7) Why do the cats 'think she is a princess out of a tower'?

(8) 'They rub at her legs for the bounty that never fails . . . .' What is 'the bounty'?

13. Rhyme

Many poems possess **rhyme**, which is usually the *similarity in the end-sounds* of words that end lines of poetry. Here's an example in which all the lines rhyme:

A YOUNG LADY OF SPAIN

There was a young lady of Sp<u>ain</u>
Who was dreadfully sick on a tr<u>ain</u>,
   Not once, but ag<u>ain</u>
    And again and ag<u>ain</u>,
And again and again and ag<u>ain</u>.

On the other hand, look at 'Henry Sutton', in which the pattern of the rhyme (also called the *rhyme-scheme*) is different:

HENRY S<u>UTTON</u>

Made his w<u>ife</u>
Serve him m<u>utton</u>
All his l<u>ife</u>.

When going to sl<u>eep</u>,
His mind was r<u>ested</u>
By counting the sh<u>eep</u>
That he'd dig<u>ested</u>!

Rhyme practice

Think up three words that rhyme with each of the following:

(1) spear ....
(2) white ....
(3) pudding ....
(4) rough ....
(5) mighty ....
(6) creep ....
(7) red ....
(8) look ....
(9) banana ....
(10) din ....

Boxes of rhymes

'Hit Tune' is a limerick from which the key rhyming words have been transferred to the box below it. Your job is to return each word correctly to its line.

HIT TUNE

There was a composer named ....
Who composed a new popular ....
    It was simply the ....
    Of a lovesick ....
With occasional thumps on the ....

| croon | gong | baboon | Bong | song |

Do the same with the limericks that follow.

THE CANNIBAL

A cannibal bold of ....
Ate an uncle and two of his ....
A cow and her ....
An ox and a ....
And now he can't button his ....

pants half aunts Penzance calf

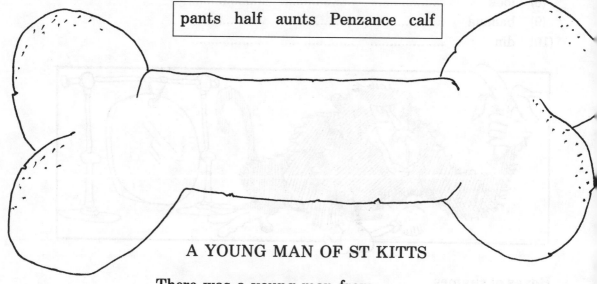

A YOUNG MAN OF ST KITTS

There was a young man from ....
Who was very much troubled with ....
    The eclipse of the ....
    Threw him into a ....
When he tumbled and broke into ....

St Kitts   moon   bits   swoon   fits

THE FAITH-HEALER

There was a faith-healer of ....
Who said: 'Although pain isn't ....
   If I sit on a ....
   And it punctures my ....
I dislike what I fancy I ....'

| real | skin | feel | Deal | pin |

THE LADY OF RYDE

There was a young lady of ....
Of eating green apples she ....
   Inside the ....
   The apples ....
And made cider inside her ....

| inside fermented Ryde lamented died |

A YOUNG PERSON

There was a young person named ....
Who dined before going to ....
   On lobster and ....
   And salad and ....
And when he awoke he was ....

| ham | dead | bed | Ned | jam |

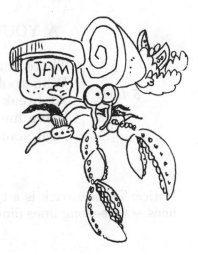

More practice

Pair off the rhyming words from the following box. You should end up with ten pairs.

weight	although	shark	plum	shiver
plate	teeth	aisle	leisure	quiver
prey	trial	neat	complete	thumb
blow	measure	dark	sleigh	beneath

What are the rhyming words in the 'Le Restaurant' comic strip, below?

The Limerick in Detail

Now that you've come across a few limericks at work, let's look at the form in more detail.

A YOUNG MAN OF CALCUTTA ← *Title*

5 lines {
There was a young man of Calcutta → *rhyme (a)*
Who spoke with a terrible stutter. → *rhyme (a)*
At breakfast he said, → *rhyme (b)*
'Give me b-b-b-bread, → *rhyme (b)*
And some b-b-b-b-b-b-butter.' → *rhyme (a)*

Notice: This limerick is a typical one. It has a title, and is made up of five lines — three long lines (lines 1, 2 and 5) and two short lines (lines 3 and 4).

The long lines have one kind of rhyme (a) and the short lines have a different rhyme (b). The rhythm and number of syllables are similar for lines 1, 2 and 5, while lines 3 and 4 also match in rhythm and are very close in syllables.

Take special note: the last line of any limerick is special because it is the funny one — the one that contains the *surprise* or *punchline*.

Limerick practice

Below are limericks that are all mixed-up. Using the guide given in the two preceding paragraphs, see if you can reconstruct them.

An Old Lady of Brooking

- She could bake sixty pies
- Without even going and looking.
- There was an old lady of Brooking,
- All quite the same size,
- Who had a great genius for cooking;

The Old Man of Hull

- He cried with despair
- Who twisted the tail of a bull.
- There was an old man from Hull
- 'That's the last stupid trick I shall pull.'
- As he flew through the air:

The Railway Official

- It cut him — it cut him in two!
- Though he smiled and he bowed,
- A railway official of Skewe
- That engine was proud;
- Met an engine one day that he knew.

A Young Lad of St Just

- Who ate apple pie till he bust;
- What finished him off was the crust.
- It wasn't the fru-it
- That caused him to do it,
- There was a young lad of St Just

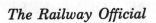

For Your Enjoyment

THE YOUNG STUDENT OF CRETE

There was a young student of Crete,
Who stood on his head in the street.
Said he, 'It is clear
If I mean to stop here
I shall have to shake hands with my feet.'

RUMBLINGS

I sat next the Duchess at tea.
It was just as I feared it would be:
  Her rumblings abdominal
  Were simply abominable,
And everyone thought it was me.

THE YOUNG BARD

There was a young bard of Japan
Whose limericks never would scan;
When they said it was so,
He replied: 'Yes, I know,
But I make a rule of always trying to get just as many
  words into the last line as I possibly can.'

THE YOUNG FELLOW

There was a young fellow of Ceuta
Who rode into church on his scooter;
He knocked down the Dean
And said: 'Sorry old bean,
I ought to have sounded my hooter.'

SHE FROWNED

She frowned and called him Mr
Because in sport he kr.
  And so, in spite,
  That very night,
This Mr kr sr.

RESPIRE, ASPIRE, SUSPIRE

There was a young girl in the choir
Whose voice arose higher and higher,
  Till one Sunday night
  It rose quite out of sight,
And they found it next day on the spire.

THE OLD LADY OF KENT

There was an old lady of Kent
Whose nose was remarkably bent.
One day, they suppose,
She followed her nose,
For no one knows which way she went.

A YOUNG MAN OF BELSIZE

There's a young man who lives in Belsize
Who believes he is clever and wise.
  Now what do you think?
  He saves gallons of ink
By simply not dotting his i's.

DO NOT SPIT

There was an old man of Darjeeling
Who travelled from London to Ealing.
  It said on the door,
  'Please don't spit on the floor',
So he carefully spat on the ceiling.

THE OLD MAN OF BLACKHEATH

There was an old man of Blackheath
Who sat on his set of false teeth.
Said he, with a start,
'O, Lord, bless my heart!
I have bitten myself underneath!'

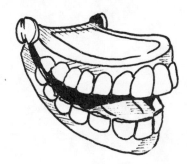

THE OLD MAN OF PERU

There was an old man of Peru
Who dreamt he was eating his shoe.
He woke in the night
In a terrible fright,
And found it was perfectly true.

THE YOUNG MAN OF DEVIZES

There was a young man of Devizes,
Whose ears were of different sizes;
  One was quite small,
  And of no use at all,
But the other was huge and won prizes.

THE OLD PERSON OF FRATTON

There was an old person of Fratton
Who would go to church with his hat on.
  'If I wake up,' he said,
  'With my hat on my head,
I shall know that it hasn't been sat on.'

14. Story-Poems

'The Inchcape Rock' is a story-poem about a man who receives his just reward for a wicked crime.

THE INCHCAPE ROCK

No stir in the air, no stir in the sea,
The ship was still as she could be,
Her sails from heaven received no motion,
Her keel was steady in the ocean.

Without either sign or sound of their shock
The waves flow'd over the Inchcape Rock;
So little they rose, so little they fell,
They did not move the Inchcape Bell.

The Abbot of Aberbrothok
Had placed that bell on the Inchcape Rock;
On a buoy in the storm it floated and swung,
And over the waves its warning rung.

When the Rock was hid by the surge's swell,
The mariners heard the warning bell;
And then they knew the perilous Rock,
And blest the Abbot of Aberbrothok.

The Sun in heaven was shining gay,
All things were joyful on that day;
The sea-birds scream'd as they wheel'd round,
And there was joyance in their sound.

The buoy of the Inchcape Bell was seen
A darker speck on the ocean green;
Sir Ralph the Rover walk'd his deck,
And he fixed his eye on the darker speck.

He felt the cheering power of spring,
It made him whistle, it made him sing;
His heart was mirthful to excess,
But the Rover's mirth was wickedness.

His eye was on the Inchcape float;
Quoth he, 'My men, put out the boat,
And row me to the Inchcape Rock,
And I'll plague the Abbot of Aberbrothok.'

The boat is lower'd, the boatmen row,
And to the Inchcape Rock they go;
Sir Ralph bent over from the boat,
And he cut the Bell from the Inchcape float.

Down sunk the Bell with a gurgling sound,
The bubbles rose and burst around;
Quoth Sir Ralph, 'The next who comes to the Rock
Won't bless the Abbot of Aberbrothok.'

Sir Ralph the Rover sail'd away,
He scour'd the seas for many a day;
And now grown rich with plunder'd store,
He steers his course for Scotland's shore.

So thick a haze o'erspreads the sky,
They cannot see the Sun on high;
The wind hath blown a gale all day,
At evening it hath died away.

On the deck the Rover takes his stand,
So dark it is they see no land.
Quoth Sir Ralph, 'It will be lighter soon,
For there is the dawn of the rising Moon.'

'Canst hear,' said one, 'the breakers roar?
For methinks we should be near the shore.'
'Now where we are I cannot tell,
But I wish I could hear the Inchcape Bell.'

They hear no sound, the swell is strong;
Though the wind hath fallen they drift along,
Till the vessel strikes with a shivering shock, —
'O Christ! it is the Inchcape Rock!'

Sir Ralph the Rover tore his hair;
He cursed himself in his despair;
The waves rushed in on every side,
The ship is sinking beneath the tide.

But even in his dying fear
One dreadful sound could the Rover hear,
A sound as if with the Inchcape Bell,
The Devil below was ringing his knell.

ROBERT SOUTHEY

The Inchcape Rock — Reading for detail

(1) Why was the Inchcape Bell not ringing when Sir Ralph first saw it?

(2) In what kind of mood was Sir Ralph?

(3) What reason did Sir Ralph give for cutting the Bell from the float?

(4) What had Sir Ralph been doing before he returned to the Inchcape Rock?

(5) How did Sir Ralph react to his ship's sinking?

(6) There is a contrast between the sea in the first scene of the poem and the sea at the end of the poem. What is it?

(7) 'The Devil below was ringing his knell.' What is the meaning of these words?

(8) Write down the stanza you liked best, and then explain why you chose it.

This is a story-poem from the American Civil War (1861–1865). It was fought between the northern and southern states, partly over the question of Negro slavery, which existed on the plantations in the South. Stonewall Jackson and Robert E. Lee were Confederate (Southern) generals. The incident described in this poem took place after the Confederate Army's victory at Fredericksburg, Virginia. The flag that Barbara Frietchie was flying was the 'Stars and Stripes', the flag of the Union (Northern) armies. It is now the United States flag. The North eventually defeated the South.

BARBARA FRIETCHIE

Up from the meadows rich with corn,
Clear in the cool September morn,

The clustered spires of Frederick stand
Green-walled by the hills of Maryland.

Round about them orchards sweep,
Apple and peach tree fruited deep,

Fair as the garden of the Lord
To the eyes of the famished rebel horde,

On that pleasant morn of the early fall
When Lee marched over the mountain-wall;

Over the mountains winding down,
Horse and foot, into Frederick town.

Forty flags with their silver stars,
Forty flags with their crimson bars,

Flapped in the morning wind: the sun
Of noon looked down, and saw not one.

Up rose old Barbara Frietchie then
Bowed with her fourscore years and ten;

Bravest of all in Frederick town.
She took up the flag the men hauled down;

In her attic window the staff she set,
To show that one heart was loyal yet.

Up the street came the rebel tread,
Stonewall Jackson riding ahead.

Under his slouched hat left and right
He glanced; the old flag met his sight.

'Halt!' — the dust-brown ranks stood fast.
'Fire! — out blazed the rifle-blast.

It shivered the window, pane and sash;
It rent the banner with seam and gash.

Quick, as it fell, from the broken staff
Dame Barbara snatched the silken scarf.

She leaned far out on the window-sill,
And shook it forth with a royal will.

'Shoot, if you must, this old grey head,
But spare your country's flag,' she said.

A shade of sadness, a blush of shame,
Over the face of the leader came;

The nobler nature within him stirred
To life at that woman's deed and word;

'Who touches a hair of yon grey head
Dies like a dog! March on!' he said.

All day long through Frederick street
Sounded the tread of marching feet:

All day long that free flag tost
Over the heads of the rebel host.

Ever its torn folds rose and fell
On the loyal winds that loved it well;

And through the hill-gaps sunset light
Shone over it with a warm good-night.

Barbara Frietchie's work is o'er,
And the Rebel rides on his raids no more.

Honour to her! and let a tear
Fall, for her sake, on Stonewall's bier.

Over Barbara Frietchie's grave,
Flag of Freedom and Union, wave!

Peace and order and beauty draw
Round thy symbol of light and law;

And ever the stars above look down
On thy stars below in Frederick town!

                    JOHN GREENLEAF WHITTIER

Barbara Frietchie — Points to consider

(1)   What impression does the poet give of Frederick town in the first
        eight lines?

(2)   What was 'the famished rebel horde'?

(3)   Why had the Union flags been hauled down?

(4)   What was Stonewall Jackson's first reaction to Barbara Frietchie's
        flag?

(5)   ' "Shoot, if you must, this old grey head, / But spare your country's
        flag," she said.' What do these words reveal about the character of
        Barbara Frietchie?

(6)   Why do you think Stonewall Jackson allowed Barbara Frietchie to
        live?

(7)   What words tell you that Stonewall Jackson had a huge army?

(8)   What do you think are the poet's feelings towards Barbara Frietchie?
        Quote a line or two as proof.

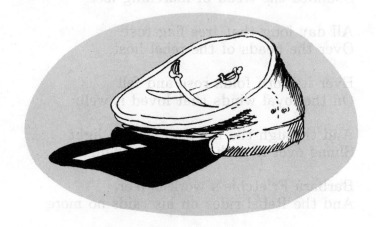

This is a poem about the greatest act of love a person can perform — the giving of his own life to save that of another.

BANNERMAN OF THE DANDENONG

I rode through the bush in the burning noon,
  Over the hills to my bride,
The track was rough and the way was long,
And Bannerman of the Dandenong,
  He rode along by my side.

A day's march off my Beautiful dwelt,
  By the Murray streams in the West;
Lightly lilting a gay love-song
Rode Bannerman of the Dandenong,
  With a blood-red rose on his breast.

'Red, red rose of the Western streams,'
  Was the song he sang that day —
Truest comrade in hour of need,
Bay Mathinna his peerless steed —
  I had my own good grey.

There fell a spark on the upland grass —
  The dry bush leapt into flame;
And I felt my heart go cold as death,
But Bannerman smiled and caught his breath,
  But I heard him name her name.

Down the hillside the fire-floods rushed,
  On the roaring eastern wind;
Neck and neck was the reckless race,
Ever the bay mare kept her pace,
  But the grey horse dropped behind.

He turned in the saddle — 'Let's change, I say!'
  And his bridle rein he drew.
He sprang to the ground, 'Look sharp!' he said
With a backward toss of his curly head —
  'I ride lighter than you!'

Down and up — it was quickly done —
　No words to waste that day!
Swift as a swallow she sped along,
The good bay mare from Dandenong,
　And Bannerman rode the grey.

The hot air scorched like a furnace blast
　From the very mouth of hell:
The blue gums caught and blazed on high
Like flaming pillars into the sky;
　The grey horse staggered and fell.

'Ride, ride, lad, ride for her sake!' he cried;
　Into the gulf of flame
Were swept, in less than a breathing space
The laughing eyes, and the comely face,
　And the lips that named *her* name.

She bore me bravely, the good bay mare;
　Stunned, and dizzy and blind;
I heard the sound of a mingling roar —
'Twas the Lachlan river that rushed before,
　And the flames that rolled behind.

Safe — safe, at Nammoora gate,
　I fell, and lay like a stone.
O love! thine arms were about me then,
Thy warm tears called me to life again,
　But — O God! that I came alone!

We dwell in peace, my beautiful one
　And I, by the streams of the West,
But oft through the mist of my dreams along
Rides Bannerman of the Dandenong
　With the blood-red rose on his breast.

ALICE WERNER

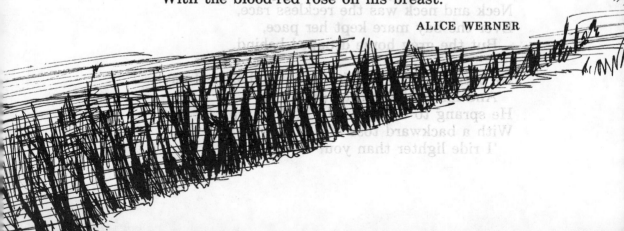

Bannerman of the Dandenong — Gaining insight into the poem

(1) Where were the narrator and Bannerman going?

(2) 'Truest comrade in hour of need . . . .' What happens in the poem to show this statement to be true?

(3) 'There fell a spark on the upland grass —' In what ways was Bannerman's reaction different from the narrator's.

(4) Why did the fire spread so rapidly?

(5) How did Bannerman convince his companion to change horses?

(6) 'Swift as a swallow' is a simile that conveys the speed of Bannerman's bay mare. Find and explain another simile in the poem.

(7) What words communicate the intense heat?

(8) 'Ride, ride, lad, ride for her sake!' Why do you think Bannerman uttered these words?

(9) How did the narrator become aware that he had reached the river?

(10) What could you say about the character of Bannerman?

The following is being told by a French soldier who, the poet would have us imagine, was actually present at the battle fought at Ratisbon in Bavaria on 23 April 1809. The French, under Napoleon, finally won the war against the Austrians. Lannes was the French marshal leading Napoleon's forces at Ratisbon.

INCIDENT OF THE FRENCH CAMP

You know, we French stormed Ratisbon:
   A mile or so away,
On a little mound, Napoleon
   Stood on our storming day;
With neck out-thrust, you fancy how,
   Legs wide, arms locked behind,
As if to balance the prone brow
   Oppressive with its mind.

Just as perhaps he mused, 'My plans
   That soar, to earth may fall,
Let once my army-leader Lannes
   Waver at yonder wall,' —
Out 'twixt the battery-smokes there flew
   A rider, bound on bound
Full-galloping; nor bridle drew
   Until he reached the mound.

Then off there flung in smiling joy,
   And held himself erect
By just his horse's mane, a boy:
   You hardly could suspect —
(So tight he kept his lips compressed,
   Scarce any blood came through)
You looked twice ere you saw his breast
   Was all but shot in two.

'Well,' cried he, 'Emperor, by God's grace
   We've got you Ratisbon!
The Marshal's in the market-place,
   And you'll be there anon
To see your flag-bird flap his vans
   Where I, to heart's desire,
Perched him!' The chief's eye flashed; his plans
   Soared up again like fire.

The chief's eye flashed; but presently
    Softened itself, as sheathes
A film the mother-eagle's eye
    When her bruised eaglet breathes;
'You're wounded!' 'Nay,' his soldier's pride
    Touched to the quick, he said:
'I'm killed, Sire!' And his chief beside,
    Smiling the boy fell dead.

                            ROBERT BROWNING

Incident of the French Camp — Quick questions

(1) Where was Napoleon while the battle was in progress?
(2) What words show that Napoleon was worried?
(3) Why was the boy holding himself by his horse's mane?
(4) Where had the boy placed the flag? How did Napoleon react to this news?
(5) Why does the poet compare the boy to a 'bruised eaglet'? What is Napoleon compared to?
(6) 'Smiling the boy fell dead.' Why was the boy smiling?

Count de Lorge's lady miscalculates when she dramatically puts his love to the test by having him retrieve her glove from the lions' den.

THE GLOVE AND THE LIONS

King Francis was a hearty king, and loved a royal sport,
And one day as his lions fought, sat looking on the court;
The nobles filled the benches, with the ladies in their pride,
And 'mongst them sat the Count de Lorge, with one for whom he sighed:
And truly 'twas a gallant thing to see that crowning show,
Valour and love, and a king above, and the royal beasts below.

Ramped and roared the lions, with horrid laughing jaws;
They bit, they glared, gave blows like beams, a wind went with their
 paws;
With wallowing might and stifled roar they rolled on one another,
Till all the pit, with sand and mane, was in a thunderous smother;
The bloody foam above the bars came whisking through the air;
Said Francis then, 'Faith, gentlemen, we're better here than there!'

De Lorge's love o'erheard the King, a beauteous, lively dame,
With smiling lips, and sharp bright eyes, which always seemed the
 same:
She thought, 'The Count, my lover, is brave as brave can be;
He surely would do wondrous things to show his love of me!
King, ladies, lovers, all look on; the occasion is divine,
I'll drop my glove to prove his love; great glory will be mine!'

She dropped her glove to prove his love: then looked at him and
 smiled;
He bowed, and in a moment leaped among the lions wild!
The leap was quick: return was quick; he has regained his place;
Then threw the glove, but not with love, right in the lady's face!
'By Heaven!' said Francis, 'rightly done!' and he rose from where he
 sat:
'No love,' quoth he, 'but vanity, sets love a task like that!'

JAMES HENRY LEIGH HUNT

The Glove and the Lions — A deadly task

(1)   What words in the first stanza show that Count de Lorge felt
      affection for his lady?

(2)   What words suggest that the lions were very dangerous?

(3)   Why did Count de Lorge's love hurl her glove into the lions' den?

(4)   How did she prompt the Count to retrieve it?

(5)   What was King Francis's attitude to the lady's testing of de Lorge's
      love for her?

(6)   What kind of man do you think de Lorge was?

15. Rhythm

Rhythm is a regular beat that runs, fast or slow, through a song, a dance, a poem or an everyday sound. The *clip-clop* of horses' hoofs beats out a regular rhythm on the road. The *clickety-clack* of train wheels beats out a faster rhythm on steel rails. The words of a poem often tell you what the rhythm in the poem represents, and allow you to form a picture in your mind which will echo the regular sound you 'hear' as you read lines with a definite rhythm.

Here are lines from several poems. These lines are famous for the connection they show between the rhythm and the subject or meaning of the poem in each case.

The two lines below are from 'Break, Break, Break' by Alfred, Lord Tennyson. Hear, in your mind, the rhythm of the sea waves' crashing fall or of their beat on the cold, grey stones.

> Break, break, break
> On thy cold grey stones, O Sea!

The regular, hard-hitting beat of horses' hoofs is both the rhythm and the subject of the following lines, from 'Song of the Cattle Hunters' by Henry Kendall.

> And the beat and the beat of our swift horses' feet
> Start the echoes away from their caves —

The swaying rhythm of the four lines below, from 'The Fighting Téméraire' by Sir Henry Newbolt, gives us a clear picture of the cheerful daily routine aboard a warship riding at anchor and swinging to the tide.

> It was eight bells ringing,
>   And the gunner's lads were singing,
> For the ship she rode a-swinging
>   As they polished every gun.

Poems with a Rhythmic Beat

Each of the following poems has a rhythmic beat. Read them to yourself, savour the rhythms, then try to identify the particular rhythm or movement used in each.

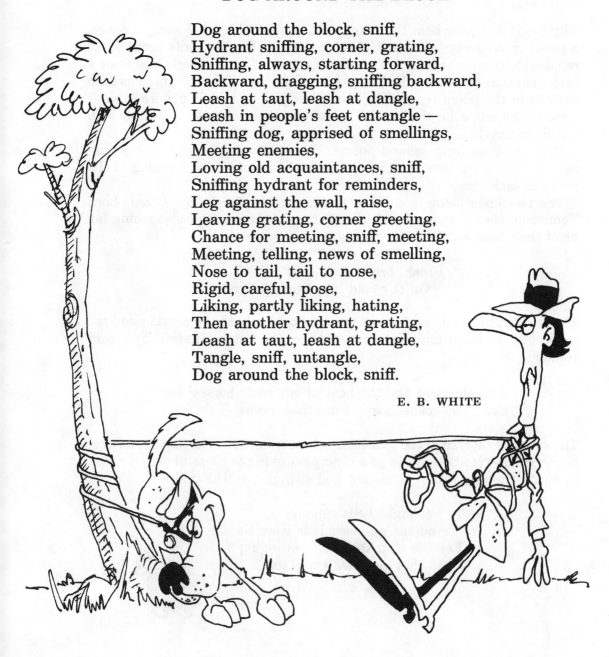

DOG AROUND THE BLOCK

Dog around the block, sniff,
Hydrant sniffing, corner, grating,
Sniffing, always, starting forward,
Backward, dragging, sniffing backward,
Leash at taut, leash at dangle,
Leash in people's feet entangle —
Sniffing dog, apprised of smellings,
Meeting enemies,
Loving old acquaintances, sniff,
Sniffing hydrant for reminders,
Leg against the wall, raise,
Leaving grating, corner greeting,
Chance for meeting, sniff, meeting,
Meeting, telling, news of smelling,
Nose to tail, tail to nose,
Rigid, careful, pose,
Liking, partly liking, hating,
Then another hydrant, grating,
Leash at taut, leash at dangle,
Tangle, sniff, untangle,
Dog around the block, sniff.

E. B. WHITE

from THE PIED PIPER OF HAMELIN

Once more he stept into the street;
And to his lips again
Laid his long pipe of smooth straight cane;
And ere he blew three notes (such sweet
Soft notes as yet musician's cunning
Never gave the enraptured air)
There was a rustling, that seemed like a bustling
Of merry crowds justling at pitching and hustling,
Small feet were pattering, wooden shoes clattering,
Little hands clapping and little tongues chattering,
And, like fowls in a farm-yard when barley is scattering,
Out came the children running.

ROBERT BROWNING

BOOTS

We're foot — slog — slog — slog — sloggin' over Africa!
Foot — foot — foot — foot — sloggin' over Africa —
(Boots — boots — boots — boots, movin' up and down again!)
        There's no discharge in the war!

Seven — six — eleven — five — nine-an'-twenty mile to-day —
Four — eleven — seventeen — thirty-two the day before —
(Boots — boots — boots — boots, movin' up and down again!)
        There's no discharge in the war!

RUDYARD KIPLING

Now let's look at a poem that is famous for its rhythm — 'Tarantella'. But first some words of explanation. The tarantella is a lively dance from southern Europe. It was once thought to be a cure for the dancing mania supposedly brought on by the bite of a tarantula spider.

This poem is about a memory. The poet thinks about a girl, Miranda, and remembers an inn by the river Aragon in the Pyrenees of Spain. These mountains, in the north-east of the country, form the border between Spain and France. The poet's memory is full of the way the inn looked, the people there, the sounds he heard with Miranda, and many other things. However, the main thing he remembers is the tarantella, and the wonderful rhythm of this dance.

TARANTELLA

Do you remember an Inn,
Miranda?
Do you remember an Inn?
And the tedding and the spreading
Of the straw for a bedding,
And the fleas that tease in the High Pyrenees,
And the wine that tasted of tar?
And the cheers and the jeers of the young muleteers
(Under the vine of the dark verandah)?
Do you remember an Inn, Miranda,
Do you remember an Inn?
And the cheers and the jeers of the young muleteers
Who hadn't got a penny,
And who weren't paying any,
And the hammer at the doors and the Din?
And the Hip! Hop! Hap!
Of the clap
Of the hands to the twirl and the swirl
Of the girl gone chancing,
Glancing,
Dancing,
Backing and advancing,
Snapping of the clapper to the spin
Out and in —
And the Ting, Tong, Tang of the Guitar!
Do you remember an Inn,
Miranda?
Do you remember an Inn?

Never more;
Miranda,
Never more.
Only the high peaks hoar:
And Aragon a torrent at the door.
No sound
In the walls of the Halls where falls
The tread
Of the feet of the dead to the ground
No sound:
But the boom
Of the far Waterfall like Doom.

HILAIRE BELLOC

Tarantella — Getting into the swing of the poem

Feeling, taste, hearing, sight — all form part of the poet's memory of the inn. See if you can identify some of the sensations by answering the following questions.

(1) What teased in the High Pyrenees?
(2) How did the wine taste?
(3) What kinds of sounds did the young muleteers make?
(4) What was seen growing over the verandah of the inn?
(5) What sound was heard at the doors of the inn?

But the inn is merely the setting for the dance. The words that introduce the actual rhythm of the dance are:

> And the Hip! Hop! Hap!
> Of the clap
> Of the hands to the twirl and the swirl

Now see if you can get into the swing of the rhythm by answering the following questions.

(6) What three words give the measured beat of handclaps?
(7) Give the two sound-words that suggest first the spinning movement of a dance and then the whirl of the dancing girl's skirt.
(8) What line suggests the snapping rhythm of the castanets as the dancer spins?
(9) Give three words that actually 'twang', like the sounds of the guitar.

When the dance is over, the mood (or feeling) of the poem changes. See if you can fit in with this change of mood by answering the following.

(10)   Why do you think the poet repeats the words 'Never more'?

(11)   What word tells you that the Aragon is a wild river?

(12)   In the last seven lines, from 'No sound', the rhythm paces slowly along to fit in with the mood (feeling) of these lines. Is the mood (a) merry (b) sad (c) bright?

(13)   What sound does the word 'boom' represent?

(14)   Why do you think there *is* such a contrast between the first part of the poem, which is all about the dance, and the last twelve lines of the poem, from 'Never more'?

Now, here is a poem you might enjoy reading aloud, and even tapping your foot to, because every line and every verse swings along with a great sense of rhythm. The subject of the poem is the Big-Brass-Band, and the poem's rhythm imitates the way the band plays as it swings along the street.

THE BAND

Hey, there! Listen awhile! Listen awhile, and come.
Down in the street there are marching feet, and I hear the beat of
   a drum.
Bim! Boom! Out of the room! Pick up your hat and fly!
Isn't it grand? The band! The band! The band is marching by!

Oh, the clarinet is the finest yet, and the uniforms are gay.
   Tah, rah! We don't go home —
   Oom, pah! We won't go home —
Oh, we shan't go home, and we *can't* go home when the band begins
   to play.

Oh, see them swinging along, swinging along the street!
Left, right! buttons so bright, jackets and caps so neat.
Ho, the Fire Brigade, or a dress parade of the Soldier-men is grand;
But everyone, for regular fun, wants a Big-Brass-Band.

The slide-trombone is a joy alone, and the drummer! He's a treat!
   So, Rackety-rumph! We don't go home —
   Boom, Bumph! We won't go home —
Oh, we shan't go home, and we *can't* go home while the band is in
   the street.

   Tooral-ooral, *Oom*-pah!
      The band is in the street!

                                        C. J. DENNIS

The Band — Did you tune in?

(1) Two things are beating out an irresistible rhythm in the first verse (stanza). Can you say what the two things are?

(2) In the second verse, words that sound like the instruments they represent blare forth. Give the sounds and say what instruments they represent.

(3) By the third verse, the band is really swinging along. What two words emphasize the swing of the legs?

(4) The fourth verse brings in the sound and rhythm of another instrument of the band. What is the instrument and what sound does it make?

Sound off!

Let's assume that there were other instruments in the band and that the poem had no time to mention them before the band had marched by. For example, there was probably a *triangle*, giving this kind of sound and rhythm:

Ding-a-ling, ding-a-ding ding!

Try assigning your own sound and rhythm to (a) cymbals (b) a kettledrum (c) a flute.

Now it's up to you to identify the rhythm in the following poem. Read the poem, then try to describe in a few words the *kind* of rhythm that seems to run through it. In what way does the rhythm of the poem add to or enhance the subject dealt with?

FROM A RAILWAY CARRIAGE

Faster than fairies, faster than witches,
Bridges and houses, hedges and ditches;
And charging along like troops in a battle,
All through the meadows, the houses and cattle;
And all of the sights of the hill and the plain
Fly as thick as driving rain;
And ever again, in the wink of an eye,
Painted stations whistle by.

Here is a child who clambers and scrambles,
All by himself and gathering brambles;
Here is a tramp who stands and gazes;
And here is the green for stringing the daisies!
Here is a cart run away in the road
Lumping along with man and load;
And here is a mill, and there is a river;
Each a glimpse and gone for ever!

ROBERT LOUIS STEVENSON

16. Poems That Mock

Sometimes, when wishing to expose human weaknesses or stupidity, a poet resorts to *satire*. The satirist tries to influence the reader in order to bring about change. Such a writer might ridicule our institutions, our attitudes or our behaviour. In 'The Unknown Citizen' W. H. Auden is satirizing the way of life of a man who never did anything wrong!

THE UNKNOWN CITIZEN

(To JS/07/M/378
This Marble Monument
Is Erected by the State)

He was found by the Bureau of Statistics to be
One against whom there was no official complaint,
And all the reports on his conduct agree
That, in the modern sense of an old-fashioned word, he was a saint,
For in everything he did he served the Greater Community.

Except for the War till the day he retired
He worked in a factory and never got fired,
But satisfied his employers, Fudge Motors Inc.
Yet he wasn't a scab or odd in his views,
For his Union reports that he paid his dues,
(Our report on his Union shows it was sound)
And our Social Psychology workers found
That he was popular with his mates and liked a drink.
The Press are convinced that he bought a paper every day
And that his reactions to advertisements were normal in every way.
Policies taken out in his name prove that he was fully insured,
And his Health-card shows he was once in hospital but left it cured.
Both Producers Research and High-Grade Living declare
He was fully sensible to the advantages of the Instalment Plan
And had everything necessary to the Modern Man,
A phonograph, a radio, a car and a frigidaire.

Our researchers into Public Opinion are content
That he held the proper opinions for the time of year;
When there was peace, he was for peace; when there was war, he
   went.
He was married and added five children to the population,
Which our Eugenist says was the right number for a parent of his
   generation,
And our teachers report that he never interfered with their edu-
   cation.
Was he free? Was he happy? The question is absurd:
Had anything been wrong, we should certainly have heard.

                                                    W. H. AUDEN

The Unknown Citizen — Looking into the poem

(1) *'To JS/07/M/378 . . .'* What comment would you make about the in-
      scription of his number rather than his name on the unknown citi-
      zen's tomb?

(2) Why do you think the State erected a monument to the unknown
      citizen?

(3) What does the line 'He worked in a factory and never got fired'
      suggest about the character of the unknown citizen?

(4) What aspects of modern life are being satirized in 'The Unknown
      Citizen'?

(5) 'Was he free? Was he happy?' Do you think the unknown citizen was
      happy and free? Give your reasons.

(6) What do you think is the poet's message to the reader in 'The Un-
      known Citizen'?

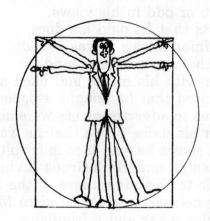

SAD SONG AT SURFER'S

Green-eyed,
tongue-tied,
skin-baked,
nose caked,
she sits, my lovely Roma
inviting carcinoma.

Whatever's nude
is 'pulchritude',
but nicely-dressed,
steam-ironed or pressed,
and topped off with a sweater —
that suits my lovely Roma better.

Truth is, I hate like hell
the barbecued and basted smell
of grilled torso and blistered thighs,
the sandy unresponsive eyes
of love quick-stricken by a coma
when I approach my lovely Roma.

Give me a mountain top
where clouds rush by and eagles flop;
but she prefers blue-bottled beaches
to bottoms bit by forest leeches;
so year by year, in 'Paradise', I dote upon my Roma,
sun-drenched, sun-drugged, inviting carcinoma.

COLIN BINGHAM

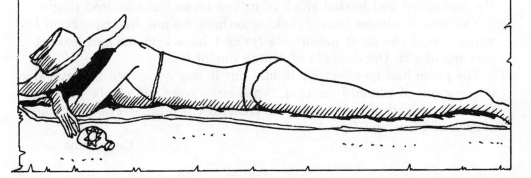

Poet's Corner

How I Came to Write 'Sad Song at Surfer's'

Friends have often asked why I wrote so passionately about my lovely Roma's contempt for carcinoma. My attitude was influenced to some extent by a hole in my left arm caused by an operation for melanoma, so skilfully performed by a Sydney surgeon that doctors in four countries, when they saw it, shouted, 'What a beauty!' or some such classical expression of approbation.

But my melanoma was not the major force in my reaction whenever I approached my green-eyed, tongue-tied, skin-baked Roma on the beach at Surfer's. That reaction was influenced by my many visits as a boy to the long beautifully curved beach in Townsville, North Queensland. It was about a mile long, and one could look out over Cleveland Bay from the marvellously sloped sand dunes, and, on a reasonably fine day, count the fins of scores of sharks waiting for intrepid bathers to be too intrepid.

If I had been older, I might have recoiled from the sight of otherwise pretty girls, disguised in the swimming suits (the men had togs) of those days, when it seemed to an observant boy that all but the female nose was well protected. When, in a few years, I had exchanged the Townsville beach for the broad flat plains of Western Queensland, I could not help deploring the inferiority of a Flinders River waterhole half-full of crocodiles to a Cleveland Bay decorated with the swiftest sharks in Christendom.

By the time I had exchanged the Outback for the coast as a place to live, the beach-dwellers of Australia had been transformed. A brief encounter with life and leeches among the mountain tops at the back of Cairns established in me a precarious preference for rugged ridges over the blue-bottled beaches, but when I fell in love with my lovely Roma, I was dismayed to find that she was perfectly at home among the barbecued and basted smell of grilled torso and blistered thighs.

This was an almost heart-breaking setback for me. In desperation I wrote one of the most passionate lyrics I have ever devised, except perhaps one on the dangers of falling out of bed.

The poem had no effect on Roma, but it was acclaimed by several doctors, one of whom, I am told, typed out a copy and displayed it on the notice board of the Townsville General Hospital, overlooking the sharks of Cleveland Bay.

Colin Bingham

In the world of buying and selling, the advertiser aims to persuade people to buy his product. The more persuasive the language, the better — even if it becomes necessary for the advertiser to create new words. In 'Superman', the poet shows us how these newly created words have become part of our language and our way of life.

SUPERMAN

I drive my car to supermarket,
The way I take is superhigh,
A superlot is where I park it,
And Super Suds are what I buy.

Supersalesmen sell me tonic —
Super-Tone-O, for Relief.
The planes I ride are supersonic.
In trains, I like the Super Chief.

Supercilious men and women
Call me superficial — me
Who so superbly learned to swim in
Supercolossality.

Superphosphate-fed foods feed me;
Superservice keeps me new.
Who would dare to supersede me,
Super-super-superwho?

JOHN UPDIKE

Superman — Words above and beyond

The prefix *super-* means 'above' or 'beyond', but in many of the recently created persuasive words it means 'outstanding' or 'exceptionally fine'.

(1) Why do you think the poem is called 'Superman'?
(2) 'Superlot' is an American 'super' word. What do you think it means?
(3) Who is likely to be responsible for the coining of a term such as 'Super Suds'?
(4) What kind of person is a superficial person?
(5) What does a supersonic plane do?
(6) 'Supercolossality' is an invented word. Guess its meaning.
(7) What does 'supersede' mean?

Writing a superpoem

Make up a 'superpoem' of your own. It should be made up only of 'super' words. Here are a few examples for a 'Super School' poem: super-teacher, superstudents, superclass, super-biro, Super Street.

'Summer Song' is a poem similar in approach to 'Superman'. What aspect of our life is the poet mocking?

SUMMER SONG

(After a surfeit of irresistible ads)

I have spot-resistant trousers,
And a crease-resistant coat,
And a wilt-resistant collar
At my thirst-resistant throat.

I've a shock-resistant wristwatch
And two leak-resistant pens,
And some sun-resistant goggles
With a glare-resistant lens.

I have scuff-resistant sneakers,
Over sweat-resistant hose,
Also run-resistant nose drops
In my pollinated nose,

And my stretch-resistant muscles
Groan in work-resistant pain
While my battered conscience tussles
With my thought-resistant brain.

W. W. WATT

Which are more important — trees or cars? Cars, of course!

'WHY DID THEY KNOCK DOWN THE TREES, DADDY?'

It's a question of standards, boy; standards of living.
It's cars, you see, that give us a high level of living —
help, so to speak, to set the thing in motion —
and if they also give us a high level of dying
that's incidental, a fringe benefit, a lottery
likely to hand out unexpected promotion.

Without cars, let's face it, a nation is under-developed,
And these days it's bad to be under-developed in anything at all —
Bust, thighs, muscles, sex or ego,
It's a competitive world, son.

The trees? Oh, well they have to go
on the advice of Big Brother
so that the cars can have a better chance
of hitting one another.

COLIN THIELE

Why *did* they knock down the trees?

(1) What reason does the father give for the knocking down of the trees?
(2) 'It's a question of standards' might be described as a kind of adult-world cliché, an empty phrase used without much thought, to answer — or to avoid *really* answering — the question put by a child. Select two other phrases from the poem which you could call adult-world clichés.
(3) 'It's cars, you see, that give us a high level of living —' Do you think cars do give us a high level of living? Explain your reasons.
(4) To what problem is the poet referring when he says that 'they also give us a high level of dying'?
(5) Who do you think 'Big Brother' is?
(6) What aspects of our way of life is the poet mocking? Why do you think he does this?

Creative Writing

(1) Try your hand at writing your own poem to answer the question 'Why did they knock down the trees, Daddy?' It could take similar lines to Colin Thiele's poem, or you could make it quite different.

OR

(2) Imagine that you are the child in this poem. You have asked your father the question 'Why did they knock down the trees, Daddy?' and have received this poem as an answer. Try your hand at shaping your thoughts now into a brief answer-poem — one that expresses some of *your* feelings and thoughts as a result of what your father has just said.

Don't forget to share your efforts with the class.

It seems that since the beginning of time the breakfast-cereal manufacturers have been including all kinds of knick-knacks in the cereal packets. The sudden onrush of miniature plastic prehistoric animals was more than this poet could bear.

ON THE INCLUSION OF MINIATURE DINOSAURS IN BREAKFAST CEREAL BOXES

A post-historic herbivore,
I come to breakfast looking for
A bite. Behind the box of Brex
I find *Tyrannosaurus rex*.

And lo! beyond the Sugar Pops,
An acetate *Triceratops*.
And here! across the Shredded Wheat,
The spoor of *Brontosaurus* feet.

Too unawake to dwell upon
A model of *Iguanodon*,
I hide within the Raisin Bran;
And thus begins the dawn of *Man*.

JOHN UPDIKE

Dinosaurs for breakfast — Over to you

(1) A herbivore is a plant-eating animal. Why does the poet refer to himself as a 'post-historic herbivore'?

(2) How does the poet create the impression that miniature plastic prehistoric animals are lying in wait for him?

17. Shapely Poems

Young people have a lot of fun reading shaped poems and creating their own for others to read and enjoy. The shape of the poem itself, or the shape it is fitted into, suggests to the reader what the poem is about. Here are some interesting shaped poems for you to read, enjoy and think about.

MOSQUITO

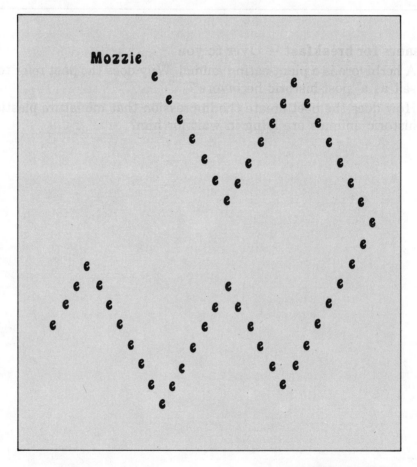

MARIE ZBIERSKI

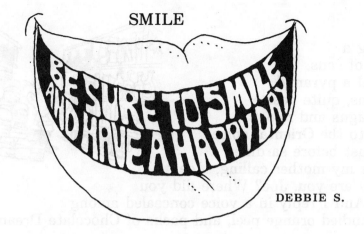

SMILE

DEBBIE S.

SAUSAGE POEM

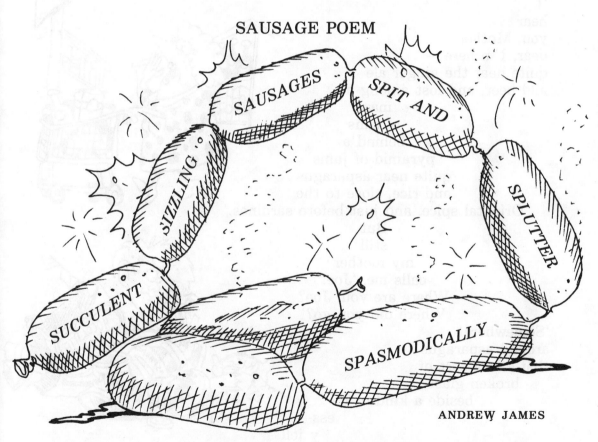

ANDREW JAMES

You've all been to the supermarket and seen the tall, precariously balanced pyramids of cans. The poet Felice Holman has converted this experience into a shaped poem for you to enjoy. Just turn the page.

SUPERMARKET

I'm
lost
among a
maze of cans,
behind a pyramid
of jams, quite near
asparagus and rice,
close to the Oriental spice,
and just before sardines.
I hear my mother calling, 'Joe.
Where are you, Joe? Where did you
Go?' And I reply in a voice concealed among
the candied orange peel, and packs of Chocolate Dreams.
'I
hear
you, Mother
dear, I'm here —
quite near the ginger ale
and beer, and lost among a
         maze
          of cans
          behind a
          pyramid of jams
         quite near asparagus
         and rice, close to the
Oriental spice, and just before sardines.'
            But
            still
          my mother
         calls me, 'Joe!
        Where are you, Joe?
        Where did you go?'
'Somewhere
around asparagus
that's in a sort of
    broken glass,
       beside a kind of m-
                ess-
              y jell
    that's near a tower of cans that f
                      e
                     l
                     l
   and squashed the Chocolate Dreams.'

FELICE HOLMAN

Shaped poems of your own

Here is a list of ideas for shaped poems of your own. See how well you can shape up.

- a kite
- a lawnmower
- a frog
- a canoe
- a syringe
- a record
- a television
- a bow and arrow

- a telephone
- a hockey stick
- a barbecue
- lightning
- a spray-can
- a trombone
- an apple
- a paperclip

- a shell
- a tyre
- a bottle
- money
- a sunset
- a slippery-dip
- a river
- a rainbow

- a surfboard
- waves
- a submarine
- an octopus
- buried treasure
- a centipede
- bubblegum
- a cup and saucer

Shaped poems of your initials

Perhaps the easiest shaped poem to write is one made up of your initials. Look at the E.T. initials below. The E is made up of **E**'s and the T is made up of **T**'s. Now, using your own initials, try the same technique.

```
EEEEEEE      TTTTTTTTTTT
E                 T
E                 T
EEEE         ·    T
E                 T
E                 T
EEEEEEE  ::       T        ::     ALLISON S.
```

Here are some more shaped poems that might give you further ideas. Can you find the *Wurm* (worm) in the *Apfel* (apple) in this German shaped poem?

APFEL

REINHARD DÖHL

RAINDROP

A drop
of water
      hit my window,
Felt the pull
to downward places —
Joined another drop —
another,
     Still one more
        and more
          until
    it
      zig-zagged
rapidly
    into a stream
      of crystal
        and ran
        to the
        bottom
        of
        the
        pane.

JOHN TRAVERS MOORE

ᴍOUSTACHE

CAROL ELLIOT

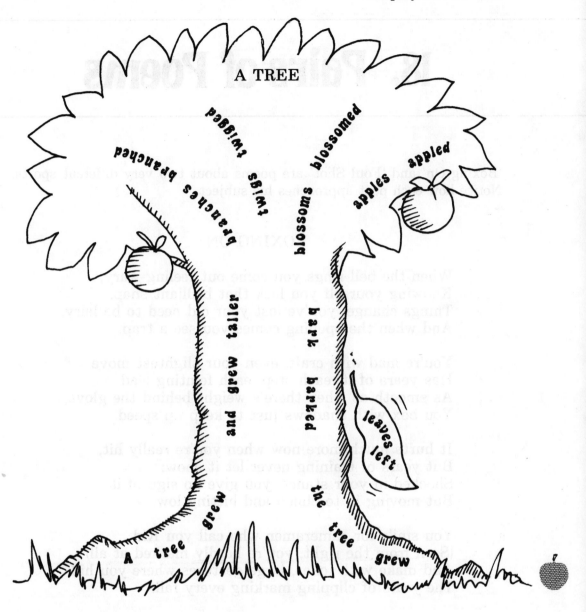

A TREE

blossomed

twigged

branched

apples

blossoms

branches

appled

bark

grew taller

barked

and

leaves left

grew

A tree

the tree grew

grew

18. Pairs of Poems

'Boxing On' and 'Foul Shot' are poems about two very different sports.
Notice how each poet approaches his subject.

BOXING ON

When the bell rings you come out feeling wary,
Knowing yourself you lack that brilliant snap.
Things change: you've lost your old need to be lairy,
And when the opening comes you see a trap.

You're mad with craft: even your slightest move
Has years of it, each step, each feinting lead
As smooth as when there's weight behind the glove;
You box with shadows just to keep up speed.

It hurts much more now when you're really hit,
But years of training never let it show:
Shocked in your stance, you give no sign of it
But moving in to clinch and hitting low.

You smile for cameramen who call you Kid
(Seen from the right, you're hardly marked at all)
And make with jokes, large gestures where you hid
The years of clipping marking every fall.

At thirty you're already getting old —
Time to hang up the gloves? That's time to kill,
Say twenty years: I'd rather take it cold,
And when I have to then I guess I will.

EVAN JONES

Boxing On — Moving in on the poem

(1) How do you know the boxer is getting old?
(2) What are some of the boxing terms used by the poet?
(3) Why do you think the poet has introduced these boxing terms into his poem?
(4) The poet could have called his poem 'Boxing'. Why is 'Boxing On' a better title?
(5) The boxer has lost 'that brilliant snap'. What has he replaced it with?
(6) What does the boxer do when he is 'really hit'?
(7) Is the name 'Kid' still appropriate to the boxer? Why?
(8) In the last stanza, what question is put to the boxer? What is his reply?

Issues for Discussion

(1) What are your feelings about boxing as a sport?
(2) Do you think boxing should be allowed to be televised? Give reasons.
(3) Do you think the sport has become over-commercialized? In what ways?

In 'Foul Shot', a single moment of high tension is taken out of a basketball game and the whole poem woven like a fabric round it. It is the crucial moment in the game, a moment when everyone's breath is held and the world seems to wait: with the score tied and time gone, a player lines up a free shot at the basket. Notice how the poet teases, making *us* wait too.

FOUL SHOT

With two 60's stuck on the scoreboard
And two seconds hanging on the clock,
The solemn boy in the centre of eyes,
Squeezed by silence,
Seeks out the line with his feet,
Soothes his hands along his uniform,
Gently drums the ball against the floor,
Then measures the waiting net,
Raises the ball on his right hand,
Balances it with his left,
Calms it with fingertips,
Breathes,
Crouches,
Waits,
And then through a stretching of stillness,
Nudges it upward.

The ball
Slides up and out,

Lands,
Leans,
Wobbles,
Wavers,
Hesitates,
Exasperates,
Plays it coy
Until every face begs with unsounding screams —
And then
    And then
      And then
Right before ROAR-UP,
Dives down and through.

EDWIN A. HOEY

Each of the next two poems gives us a description of a father, and of his relationship with his family.

OUR FATHER

She said my father had whiskers and looked like God;
that he swore like a fettler, drank like a bottle;
used to run away from mother, left money for food;
called us by numbers; had a belt with a buckle.

On Sunday was churchday. We children walked behind.
He'd wear a stiff collar. He'd say good-morning.
And we made jokes about him, we were afraid
because already we understood about hating.

When we'd left the church that was so nice and still,
the minister would let us give the bells a telling —
four dong-dells; and we'd decide that Nell's
was to be the end of the world; it was time for going.

When we got home he'd take off his collar, and his shoes;
and his Sunday-special braces; and we'd whisper,
he's not like God. So that he'd belt us for the noise,
and we'd yell. And on Mondays he'd run away from mother.

RAY MATHEW

THOSE WINTER SUNDAYS

Sundays too my father got up early
and put his clothes on in the blueblack cold,
then with cracked hands that ached
from labor in the weekday weather made
banked fires blaze. No one ever thanked him.

I'd wake and hear the cold splintering, breaking.
When the rooms were warm, he'd call,
and slowly I would rise and dress,
fearing the chronic angers of that house,

Speaking indifferently to him,
who had driven out the cold
and polished my good shoes as well.
What did I know, what did I know
of love's austere and lonely offices?

ROBERT HAYDEN

Two fathers and five questions

Draw up the following table in your workbook and insert the answers to
the questions that follow.

	'Our Father'	'Those Winter Sundays'
(1)		
(2)		
(3)		
(4)		
(5)		

(1) What was one of the most noticeable things about each father?
(2) How did each father treat his children/child?
(3) How did the children/child react to the father's treatment?
(4) What are your feelings towards each of the fathers?
(5) Why do you think the poets, Ray Mathew and Robert Hayden, wrote
these poems about their fathers?

'The Frog Pool' describes the frogs' reactions to the ending of the drought, while 'At the Pool' takes a glimpse at nature's law of survival in a lily pool.

THE FROG POOL

Week after week it shrank and shrank
As the fierce drought fiend drank and drank,
Till on the bone-dry bed revealed
the mud peeled;
But now tonight is steamy-warm,
Heavy with hint of thunderstorm.

And hark! hark! hoarse and harsh
The throaty croak of frogs in the marsh:
'Wake! wake! awake! awake!
The drought break!'
But no, that chorus seems to me
More a primeval harmony.

The thunder booms, the floods flow
Blended with deeper din below,
And every time the skies crash
The swamps flash!
And the whole place will be tonight
A pandemonium of delight.

JAMES DEVANEY

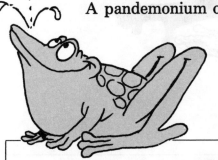

Poet's Corner

During my many years in the far interior it was always amazing to me how the frogs appeared after long spells of drought. They must have been very deep underground, the surface often being too hot to touch with the hand. On hearing them on this occasion I imagined the 'words' they seemed to be saying, and the first lines written of the poem were 'Wake, wake,' and so on.

James Devaney

AT THE POOL

I saw the way the butterfly
Came to my lily pool to die:
He sat with all his glories spread
Upon a golden seedum head
And acted all the world like one
Whose beauty could delay the sun.
Then leapt my bullfrog from the water,
As black as Ethiopian's daughter
And like what might be her desire,
He took in one quick tongue of fire
The butterfly. And that was all,
Except that close beside the wall
I later saw a bulgy eye
Watching for the next butterfly.

ERNEST G. MOLL

Poet's Corner

'At the Pool' is an observation recorded without comment and in a language that attempts to be as simple as the event itself. That simplicity is part of the terrifying beauty of nature: pure, uncomplicated instinct manifesting itself in an act essential for survival. Something lives *because* something has died — and both are beautiful.

Ernest G. Moll

Here are two poems about death. Nancy Cato is far more sympathetic to her dead swagman than Tony Connor seems to be towards Alfred Hubbard, the dead plumber.

DEAD SWAGMAN

His rusted billy left beside the tree;
Under a root, most carefully tucked away,
His steel-rimmed glasses folded in their case
Of mildewed purple velvet; there he lies
In the sunny afternoon, and takes his ease,
Curled like a possum within the hollow trunk.

He came one winter evening when the tree
Hunched its broad back against the rain, and made
His camp, and slept, and did not wake again.
Now white ants make a home within his skull:
His old friend Fire has walked across the hill
And blackened the old tree and the old man
And buried him half in ashes where he lay.

It might be called a lonely death. The tree
Led its own alien life beneath the sun,
Yet both belonged to the Bush, and now are one:
The roots and bones lie close among the soil,
And he ascends in leaves towards the sky.

NANCY CATO

Dead Swagman — Feeling the poem

(1) What clues in the poem tell you that the swagman has been dead for some time?

(2) Why do you think the poet refers to Fire as the swagman's 'old friend'?

(3) How has the poet personified the tree?

(4) 'It might be called a lonely death.' Is this your view? Why or why not?

(5) 'And he ascends in leaves towards the sky.' What explanation can you give for this surprising statement?

(6) Write down a line or two from the poem which you found especially sad, and then explain your choice.

ELEGY FOR ALFRED HUBBARD

Hubbard is dead, the old plumber;
who will mend our burst pipes now,
the tap that has dripped all the summer,
testing the sink's overflow?

No other like him. Young men with knowledge
of new techniques, theories from books,
may better his work straight from college,
but who will challenge his squint-eyed looks

in kitchen, bathroom, under floorboards,
rules of thumb which were often wrong;
seek as erringly stopcocks in cupboards,
or make a job last half as long?

He was a man who knew the ginnels,
alleyways, streets, — the whole district;
family secrets, minor annals,
time-honoured fictions fused to fact.

Seventy years of gossip muttered
under his cap, his tufty thatch,
so that his talk was slow and clotted,
hard to follow, and too much.

As though nothing fell, none vanished,
and time were the maze of Cheetham Hill,
in which the dead, — with jobs unfinished —,
waited to hear him ring the bell.

For much he never got round to doing,
but meant to, when the weather bucked up,
or worsened, or when his pipe was drawing,
or when he'd finished this cup.

I thought time, he forgot so often,
had forgotten him, but here's Death's pomp
over his house, and by the coffin
the son who will inherit his blowlamp,

tools, workshop, cart, and cornet,
(pride of Cheetham Prize Brass Band), —
and there's his mourning widow, Janet,
stood at the gate he'd promised to mend.

Soon he will make his final journey;
shaved and silent, strangely trim,
with never a pause to talk to any-
body: how arrow-like, for him!

In St Mark's Church, — whose dismal tower
he pointed and painted when a lad —,
they will sing his praises amidst flowers,
while, somewhere, a cellar starts to flood,

and the housewife banging his front-door knocker
is not surprised to find him gone,
and runs for Thwaite, who's a better worker,
and sticks at a job until it's done.

TONY CONNOR

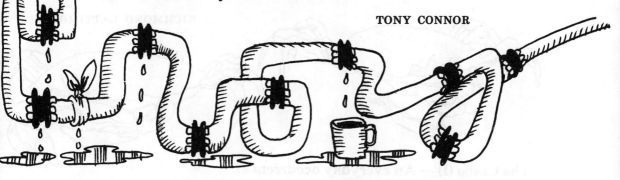

Elegy for Alfred Hubbard — Sadly missed?

(1) An elegy is a poem of mourning in which the life of the dead person is sadly recalled. In two or three sentences, write down what you learnt about Alfred Hubbard's life.

(2) What indications can you find to show that Alfred was not a very good plumber?

(3) What was Albert's attitude to time?

(4) 'Soon he will make his final journey....' What is Albert's final journey?

(5) What does 'the gate he'd promised to mend' reveal about Albert's character?

(6) What is the housewife's attitude to Albert's death?

The next two poems are not just about crabs. They both have important things to say about human beings.

THE CRABS

There was a bucket full of them. They spilled,
crawled, climbed, clawed: slowly tossed
and fell: precision made: cold iodine color of their own
world of sand and occasional brown weed, round stone
chilled clean in the chopping waters of their coast.
One fell out. The marine thing on the grass
tried to trundle off, barbarian and immaculate and to be killed
with his kin. We lit water: dumped the living mass
in: contemplated tomatoes and corn: and with the good cheer of
   civilized man,
cigarettes, that is, and cold beer, and chatter,
waited out and lived down the ten-foot-away clatter
of crabs as they died for us inside their boiling can.

RICHMOND LATTIMORE

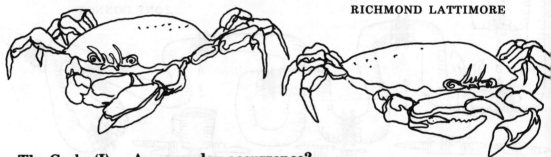

The Crabs (I) — An everyday occurrence?

(1) What words show the crabs' desperate attempts to escape from the bucket?

(2) What colour are the crabs? How does this help them in their natural environment?

(3) 'The marine thing on the grass....' What word in the next line carries on the idea that the crab is out of its natural environment?

(4) What word suggests the sound of the crabs in the can? What word represents the sound of the men talking to each other?

(5) What criticism of himself and his friends do you think the poet is making in the poem?

(6) What does the poet mean by 'they died for us'?

(7) What is your attitude to the poet and his friends?

(8) What are your feelings towards the crabs?

THE CRABS

The crabs are lunching:
An hour I've watched, and still they eat,
Pincering microcosms from the scaly rocks,
Timed to split-second mouth shutterings
Like Chinamen with chop-sticks;
No disrespect, but Asian they look,
And I on an overleaning rock am humbled.

Such industry is not mine,
Such battering I could not suffer.
The waves hiss and bury the feeders three feet deep,
Avalanches fall on their apparent frailty.
The rock bares, the sea sucks back,
And I laugh to see the crabs uninterruptedly feeding:
The littlest baby crab holds miraculously rock fast,
Centuried to sea-wash,
Insolently safe, insolently chop-stick lunching
Against the might of the sea.

I laugh, knowing crabs wiser than man;
When man, suicided from his home, the earth,
Shall see no lord sun spray gold on wave,
Nor moons come like vespers, go in full song,
Crabs still will ply their chop-sticks,
Knowing nor caring that man is dust.

BRIAN VREPONT

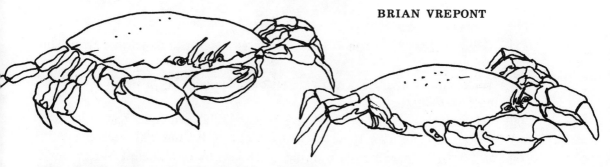

The Crabs (II) — A sobering thought?
(1) What are the crabs doing while the poet is watching them?
(2) Do you think the simile 'Like Chinamen with chop-sticks' is a good one? Give reasons.
(3) Why is the poet 'humbled' watching the crabs?
(4) Explain what the poet means by 'Such industry is not mine'.

(5) What words bring to mind the sound the sea makes?

(6) What is the meaning of 'rock fast'?

(7) What words of the poet point out that the crabs have been defying the sea for hundreds and hundreds of years?

(8) 'When man, suicided from his home, the earth . . . .' Can you suggest in what ways this might happen?

(9) What words in the last stanza suggest that the crabs will outlast man?

(10) What is the poet's attitude to the crabs?

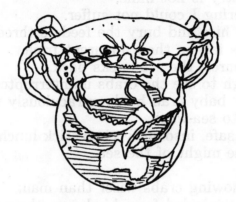

19. Alliteration and Assonance

Alliteration

In everyday living we are surrounded by things we hear and things we read in which certain letters are repeated — often to catch our attention. This device is called **alliteration**. Nursery rhymes thrive on it, as in the following:

- Wee Willie Winkie ...
- Goosey, goosey gander ...
- Baa, baa, black sheep ...

Tongue-twisters also make great use of alliteration:

A tutor who tooted the flute
Tried to tutor two tooters to toot.
Said the two to the tutor
'Is it harder to toot, or
To tutor two tooters to toot?'

And advertisers often use alliteration to make sure you get the message — and remember it!

- Don't miss the stirring saga of the pride and passions of an incredible family.
- The cold, crisp taste of Coke.
- Tennis makes you trim, taut and terrific.

An excellent exercise

(1) Make up five advertising slogans of your own which are catchy and snappy, thanks to alliteration.

(2) Some names are alliterative — e.g. Mandrake the Magician, King Kong, Sindbad the Sailor. See if you can think of other names that use alliteration. If you can't find any famous ones, create your own!

Here's a poem that is brimming and bursting with alliteration. In fact, it could hardly exist without it!

SIR SAMUEL AND SIR SILAS

Sir Samuel saw Sir Silas Simmonds swimming,
Sir Samuel saw Sir Silas Simmonds sinking.
Sir Samuel swam swift, steady strokes,
Saved Sir Silas Simmonds.
Sir Samuel said to Sir Silas,
'Say something, Silas, sir, say something'.
Sir Silas, saved, sat still and said,
'S . . s . . sorry, Sir Samuel, so s . . s . . s . . s . . s . . s . . sorry!'

Now you're ready for the kind of definition of alliteration that you can apply to more thoughtful poetry:

DEFINITION: Alliteration is the deliberate repetition of consonant-sounds to achieve a desired effect.

In the following famous verse, from Longfellow's 'The Village Blacksmith', the sounds that form the alliterations are in heavy type.

> Under a spreading chestnut-tree
> The village smithy stands;
> The smith, a mighty man is he,
> With large and sinewy hands;
> And the muscles of his brawny arms
> Are strong as iron bands.

The consonants 's', 't', 'm' and 'b' are strong and hard sounds and their repetition gives strength to this verse. This, in turn, fits in well with the picture conjured up of a hard, tough man — the iron-muscled village blacksmith at his place of work.

Finding the alliteration

In each of the following extracts from poems there is an obvious use of alliteration. Copy each extract into your workbook and underline the letters that form the alliteration.

(1) Nothing older than stone but the soil and the sea and the sky.
Nothing stronger than stone but water and air and fire.
['The Mason' by Robert Farren]

(2) The day was clear as fire,
the birds sang frail as glass,
when thirsty I came to the creek
and fell by its side in the grass.
['The Killer' by Judith Wright]

(3) Full fathom five thy father lies;
Of his bones are coral made;
[*The Tempest* by William Shakespeare]

(4) The wind was a torrent of darkness among the gusty trees,
The moon was a ghostly galleon tossed upon cloudy seas,
The road was a ribbon of moonlight over the purple moor,
['The Highwayman' by Alfred Noyes]

(5) To sit in solemn silence
In a dull, dark dock,
In a pestilential prison
With a life-long lock;
Awaiting the sensation
Of a short, sharp shock,
From a cheap and chippy chopper
On a big, black block!
[W. S. Gilbert — from *The Mikado*]

(6) A pleasant shady place it is, a pleasant place and cool —
The township folk go up and down, the children pass to school
['Old Granny Sullivan' by John Shaw Neilson]

(7) Smells rich and rasping, smoke, fat and fish
And puffs of paraffin that crimp the nose
['William Street' by Kenneth Slessor]

(8) Down came the storm, and smote amain
The vessel in its strength;
She shuddered and paused, like a frighted steed,
Then leaped her cable's length.
['The Wreck of the Hesperus' by Henry W. Longfellow]

(9)   The roving breezes come and go, the reed beds sweep and sway,
      The sleepy river murmurs low, and loiters on its way,
      It is the land o' lots of time along the Castlereagh.
                    ['The Travelling Post Office' by A. B. Paterson]

(10) Hauled headlong starward by the quadruple conviction
      Of lion-lunged engines in their pride of power
      That roar for their prey on the fleecy cloud-veldt —
      The droves of distance and the dwindling hour,
                    ['Flying to New Zealand' by Michael Thwaites]

Assonance

Now let's turn from alliteration to another sound-device used in poetry:
assonance.

> DEFINITION: Assonance is the repetition of the same vowel-sounds
> followed by different consonant-sounds.

Proverbs sometimes make use of assonance. For example:

> A stitch in <u>time</u> saves <u>nine</u>.

In poetry, assonance is one of the commonest methods of achieving a
musical effect. The following lines are from 'The Lotos-Eaters' by Alfred,
Lord Tennyson.

> There is sweet music here that softer falls
> Than petals from bl<u>o</u>wn r<u>o</u>ses on the grass,

Identifying assonance

Underline the assonance in the following extracts from poems.

(1)   And in the stream the long-leaved flowers weep,
      And from the craggy ledge the poppy hangs in sleep.
                    ['The Lotos-Eaters' by Alfred, Lord Tennyson]

(2)   With fingers weary and worn,
      With eyelids heavy and red,
                    ['The Song of the Shirt' by Thomas Hood]

(3) Nothing is so beautiful as Spring —
When weeds, in wheels, shoot long and lovely and lush;
Thrush's eggs look like little low heavens, and thrush
Through the echoing timber does so rinse and wring
The ear, it strikes like lightnings to hear him sing;
['Spring' by Gerard Manley Hopkins]

Lovely Sights and Sounds in a Famous Poem

This poem uses many beautiful sound-combinations to achieve the desired effects in describing where and how the bell-birds live and contribute to the sights and sounds of the deep mountain valleys

BELL-BIRDS

By channels of coolness the echoes are calling,
And down the dim gorges I hear the creek falling:
It lives in the mountain where moss and the sedges
Touch with their beauty the banks and the ledges.
Through breaks of the cedar and sycamore bowers
Struggles the light that is love to the flowers;
And, softer than slumber, and sweeter than singing,
The notes of the bell-birds are running and ringing.

The silver-voiced bell-birds, the darlings of daytime!
They sing in September their songs of the May-time;
When shadows wax strong, and the thunder-bolts hurtle,
They hide with their fear in the leaves of the myrtle;
When rain and the sunbeams shine mingled together,
They start up like fairies that follow fair weather;
And straightway the hues of their feathers unfolden
Are the green and the purple, the blue and the golden.

October, the maiden of bright yellow tresses,
Loiters for love in these cool wildernesses;
Loiters, knee-deep, in the grasses, to listen,
Where dripping rocks gleam and the leafy pools glisten:
Then is the time when the water-moons splendid
Break with their gold, and are scattered or blended
Over the creeks, till the woodlands have warning
Of songs of the bell-bird and wings of the Morning.

Welcome as waters unkissed by the summers
Are the voices of bell-birds to thirsty far-comers.
When fiery December sets foot in the forest,
And the need of the wayfarer presses the sorest,
Pent in the ridges for ever and ever
The bell-birds direct him to spring and to river,
With ring and with ripple, like runnels whose torrents
Are toned by the pebbles and leaves in the currents.

Often I sit, looking back to a childhood,
Mixt with the sights and the sounds of the wildwood,
Longing for power and the sweetness to fashion,
Lyrics with beats like the heart-beats of Passion; —
Songs interwoven of lights and of laughters
Borrowed from bell-birds in far forest-rafters;
So I might keep in the city and alleys
The beauty and strength of the deep mountain valleys;
Charming to slumber the pain of my losses
With glimpses of creeks and a vision of mosses.

HENRY KENDALL

Bell-Birds — The sights and the sounds

(1)   What obvious alliteration occurs in the opening lines of the poem?

(2)   The first stanza deals with the echoes heard in the deep mountain valleys. What rhyming words help you to 'hear' these echoes?

(3)   'Through breaks of the cedar and sycamore bowers / Struggles the light . . . .' Why does the light struggle?

(4)   A low but insistent alliteration runs through the lines that end the first stanza. What letters does it dwell upon?

(5)   Can you suggest why the poet chose to weave alliteration into these lines?

(6)   What example of personification can you find in the third stanza?

(7)   What alliteration can you find at the end of the third stanza which spills over into the next stanza as well?

(8)   What example of personification can you find in the fourth stanza?

(9)   'With ring and with ripple, like runnels whose torrents / Are toned by the pebbles and leaves in the currents.' In these two lines assonance and alliteration are interwoven to form a lovely mingling of sounds. Keeping in mind the sense of what is written, explain what kind of sights and sounds are conjured up in your imagination.

(10)   What is the poet contemplating in the last stanza?

20. Our Environment

What complaint against his environment is the poet making in 'Song of the Open Road'?

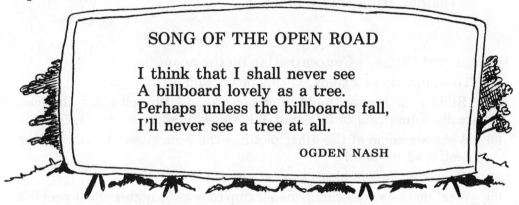

SONG OF THE OPEN ROAD

I think that I shall never see
A billboard lovely as a tree.
Perhaps unless the billboards fall,
I'll never see a tree at all.

OGDEN NASH

'Beleaguered' means 'under siege' or 'surrounded by an enemy force'. As you read the poem 'Beleaguered Cities', you will see that nature is the besieging force. Nature has been overwhelmed in the human cities by bricks and mortar — yet the existence of even a single, tiny blade of grass is enough to herald the inevitable victory of nature in the end.

BELEAGUERED CITIES

Build your houses, build your houses, build your towns,
    Fell the woodland, to a gutter turn the brook,
Pave the meadows, pave the meadows, pave the downs,
    Plant your bricks and mortar where the grasses shook,
    The wind-swept grasses shook.
Build, build your Babels black against the sky —
But mark yon small green blade, your stones between,
    The single spy
Of that uncounted host you have outcast;
For with their tiny pennons waving green
    They shall storm your streets at last.

Build your houses, build your houses, build your slums,
   Drive your drains where once the rabbits used to lurk,
Let there be no song there save the wind that hums
   Through the idle wires while dumb men tramp to work,
   Tramp to their idle work.
Silent the siege; none notes it; yet one day
Men from your walls shall watch the woods once more
   Close round their prey.
Build, build the ramparts of your giant-town;
Yet they shall crumble to the dust before
   The battering thistle-down.

F. L. LUCAS

Beleaguered Cities — Concentrating on the poem

(1)   To whom, do you think, is this poem addressed?

(2)   'Build your houses, build your houses . . . .' Do you think the poet really wants this to be done? Why or why not?

(3)   What are some of the other pictures the poet gives of nature being destroyed by man?

(4)   What are 'Babels black against the sky'?

(5)   What do the words 'dumb men tramp to work' suggest about people's attitude to work?

(6)   The poet believes that nature will eventually overcome what humans construct. What evidence in the poem can you find for this belief?

(7)   The poet uses battle terms to portray nature's victory. Jot down one or two of these that you have not used before.

(8)   Thistle-down is the light, feathery 'seeds' of the thistle. Can you suggest why the poet has called the thistle-down 'battering'?

(9)   Beleaguered cities are cities surrounded by enemy troops. Do you think the poem's title is appropriate? Why or why not?

(10) Do you agree with the poet's feelings? Give your reasons.

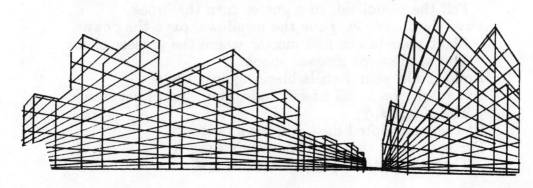

'Little Boxes' satirizes the conformity and uniformity of people's lives in today's society. People live in the same kinds of houses, they look the same, and they do the same kinds of things.

LITTLE BOXES

Little boxes on the hillside, little boxes made of ticky-tacky,
Little boxes, little boxes, little boxes all the same;
There's a green one and a pink one and a blue one and a yellow one,
And they're all made out of ticky-tacky
And they all look just the same.

And the people in the houses all go to the university,
And they all get put in boxes, little boxes, all the same;
And there's doctors and there's lawyers and business executives,
And they're all made out of ticky-tacky
And they all look just the same.

And they all play on the golf course and drink their martini dry,
And they all have pretty children and the children go to school;
And the children go to summer camp and then to the university,
And they all get put in boxes
And they all come out the same.

And the boys go into business and marry and raise a family,
And they all get put in boxes, little boxes, all the same;
There's a green one and a pink one and a blue one and a yellow one,
And they're all made out of ticky-tacky
And they all look just the same.

M. REYNOLDS
(Sung by Pete Seeger)

Here is a poem full of sadness at the destruction of a stand of pine trees
that will be badly missed in a number of important ways.

THEY HAVE CUT DOWN THE PINES

They have cut down the pines where they stood;
The wind will miss them — the rain,
When its silver blind is down.
They have stripped the bark from the wood —
The needly boughs, and the brown
Knobbly nuts trodden into the ground.
The kind, the friendly trees,
Where all day small winds sound,
And all day long the sun
Plays hide and seek with shadows
Till the multiplying shadows turn to one
And night is here.

They have cut down the trees and ended now
The gentle colloquy of bough and bough.
They are making a fence by the creek,
And have cut down the pines for the posts.
Wan in the sunlight as ghosts
The naked trunks lie.
A bird nested there — it will seek
In vain: they have cut down the pines.

MARY LISLE

They Have Cut Down the Pines — Probing the poem

(1) Why do you think the poet repeats the words 'they have cut down the pines'?

(2) What picture of the rain do the words 'its silver blind is down' give you?

(3) What do you understand by 'needly boughs' and 'Knobbly nuts'?

(4) 'The kind, the friendly trees . . . .' What human qualities do the trees possess?

(5) Explain how the poet has personified (given human qualities to) the sun.

(6) Why were the trees cut down?

(7) The word 'colloquy' means 'conversation'. Explain the meaning of 'The gentle colloquy of bough and bough'.

(8) How has the cutting down of the trees affected nature?

(9) What is the poet's message to the reader?

(10) What are your feelings about the cutting down of the pines?

'Harvest Hymn' bitterly criticizes the way we sacrifice nature and the land in our pursuit of wealth.

HARVEST HYMN

We spray the fields and scatter
    The poison on the ground
So that no wicked wild flowers
    Upon our farm be found.
We like whatever helps us
    To line our purse with pence;
The twenty-four-hour broiler-house
    And neat electric fence.

    All concrete sheds around us
      And Jaguars in the yard,
    The telly lounge and deep-freeze
      Are ours from working hard.

We fire the fields for harvest,
    The hedges swell the flame,
The oak trees and the cottages
    From which our fathers came.
We give no compensation,
    The earth is ours today,
And if we lose on arable,
    Then bungalows will pay.

    All concrete sheds around us
      And Jaguars in the yard,
    The telly lounge and deep-freeze
      Are ours from working hard.

JOHN BETJEMAN

'Coverings' is made up of two parts. In part I we are presented with a beautiful portrait of a snake. It is a snake that has newly shed its skin and so is shining 'like watered silk'. At the end of part I the reason for the wonderfully strange markings on the snake's skin is explained.

In part II of the poem we switch abruptly from the snake to a human being, a Mrs Fand, who wears or carries adornments for the making of which certain innocent creatures had to be hunted and killed. In spite of the adornments, however, Mrs Fand is an unattractive sight.

The last stanza brings both parts of the poem together because we discover that Mrs Fand is actually watching the snake.

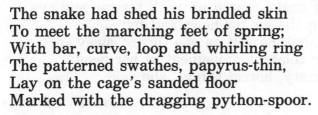

COVERINGS

I

The snake had shed his brindled skin
To meet the marching feet of spring;
With bar, curve, loop and whirling ring
The patterned swathes, papyrus-thin,
Lay on the cage's sanded floor
Marked with the dragging python-spoor.

Flick-flack! Like ash or vulcanite
His lidless eyes in the spatulate
Head were alive with watchful hate,
Daring the sounds and the raw spring light.
He shone like watered silk from his tongue
To his tapering tail where the skin-shreds hung.

The cloudy yellow of mustard flowers
Was barred on his skin with jetty flares
And the five-patched circle the leopard wears:
The sea-shell's convolute green towers
Were called to mind by his belly's hue
That faded to pallid egg-shell blue.

He was covered so to face the sun;
That shadows of leaves might match his skin;
That, where the lily roots begin,
You might not see where the snake begun;
That Man might see, when Snake was dressed,
God in snake made manifest.

II

Mrs Fand wore a fox round her wrinkled throat;
He was killed at dawn as he snarled his threat
In a bracken-brake where the mist lay wet.
Two men were drowned in a shattered boat
Hunting the whale for the silk-bound shred
That balanced her bust with her henna'd head.

An osprey's plume brushed her fallen chin,
And a lorgnette hung on a platinum chain
To deputise for her sightless brain.
Her high-heeled shoes were of python skin,
Her gloves of the gentle reindeer's hide,
And to make her card-case a lizard died.

She watched the flickering counter-play
As the snake reared up with tongue and eye
Licking the air for newt and fly;
And shook herself as she turned away
With a tolerant movement of her head:
'The nasty, horrid thing!' she said.

STELLA GIBBONS

Coverings — Examining the poem

(1)   Why do you think the poem is called 'Coverings'?
(2)   What do the words 'the marching feet of spring' mean? Explain how spring has been given human qualities.
(3)   What evidence can you find to suggest that the snake could be dangerous?
(4)   What are 'The patterned swathes, papyrus-thin'?
(5)   In what ways is the snake a beautiful creature?
(6)   What words of the poet show that Mrs Fand is physically unattractive?
(7)   'To deputise for her sightless brain.' What criticism is the poet making of Mrs Fand?
(8)   'The nasty, horrid thing!' What does this statement reveal about Mrs Fand?
(9)   What is the poet's message to the reader?
(10) What are your feelings towards (a) the snake (b) Mrs Fand?

Jigsaws are all about adding pieces to other pieces so that the construction becomes more and more extensive. This is more or less what is happening, property-wise, in the poem below.

JIGSAWS

Property! Property! Let us extend
Soul and body without end:
A box to live in, with airs and graces
A box on wheels that shows its paces,
A box that talks or that makes faces,
And curtains and fences as good as the neighbours'
To keep out the neighbours and keep us immured
Enjoying the cold canned fruit of our labours
In a sterilized cell, unshared, insured.

LOUIS MACNEICE

Jigsaws — Identify the boxes

Name the three boxes mentioned by the poet:
  (a) a box to live in, with airs and graces, is a ....
  (b) a box on wheels that shows its paces is a ....
  (c) a box that talks or that makes faces is a ....

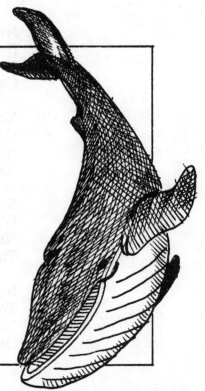

THE LAST WHALE

the solitude of water
drove him mad

he wallowed like a zeppelin
full of holes

and when he landed
on the beach

they say he made
a thousand packs

of lightly salted
margarine

MILES GIBSON

The Last Whale — Ask yourself

(1)   Why was there 'the solitude of water'?

(2)   What effect did this solitude have on the whale?

(3)   Why is the comparison of a whale to a zeppelin an apt (fitting) one?

(4)   Why is what ultimately happened to the whale so terrible?

(5)   Now ask yourself: Is there any possibility of the events presented in the poem actually coming true? Why or why not?

No more. These two words are used frequently in the following poem because the poem is partly about how things used to be in the days when the continent of Australia was peopled only by Aborigines. But big changes came with the Europeans and, as Kath Walker points out, these changes have led to all kinds of complications for the Aboriginal people.

NO MORE BOOMERANG

No more boomerang
No more spear;
Now all civilized —
Colour bar and beer.

No more corroboree,
Gay dance and din.
Now we got movies,
And pay to go in.

No more sharing
What the hunter brings.
Now we work for money,
Then pay it back for things.

Now we track bosses
To catch a few bob,
Now we go walkabout
On bus to the job.

One time naked,
Who never knew shame;
Now we put clothes on
To hide whatsaname.

No more gunya,
Now bungalow,
Paid by higher purchase
In twenty year or so.

Lay down the stone axe,
Take up the steel,
And work like a nigger
For a white man meal.

No more firesticks
That made the whites scoff.
Now all electric,
And no better off.

Bunyip he finish,
Now got instead
White fella Bunyip,
Call him red.

Abstract picture now —
What they coming at?
Cripes, in our caves we
Did better than that.

Black hunted wallaby,
White hunt dollar;
White fella witch-doctor
Wear dog-collar.

No more message-stick;
Lubras and lads
Got television now,
Mostly ads.

Lay down the woomera,
Lay down the waddy.
Now we got atom-bomb,
End *every*body.

KATH WALKER

No More Boomerang — Past and present

On the left in the table below are words from the Aborigines' way of life of the past. From the poem 'No More Boomerang', select the corresponding word that relates to the Aborigines' way of life in a European society. The first one has been done to help you.

The Aborigines' Past	White Society Now
corroboree	.... *movies* ....
sharing	....
naked	....
gunya	....
stone axe	....
firesticks	....
Bunyip	....
cave pictures	....
wallaby	....
message-stick	....
woomera	....

Thinking about the poem

(1)   Why do you think Kath Walker wrote 'No More Boomerang'?

(2)   Do you agree with her viewpoint? Give your reasons.

21. About War

The Crimean War (1853–1856) was fought between Russia on the one hand and Britain, France and Turkey on the other. The Charge of the Light Brigade occurred in November 1854 at Balaclava in the Crimea (the Black Sea area of Russia). It was led by the Earl of Cardigan. Some six hundred British cavalrymen took part in the charge. Each cavalryman was a lightly equipped soldier on horseback. The sabre, or curved sword, was an important weapon.

The brave six hundred rode straight down a valley that was fortified at its end by many cannon served by Russian and Cossack gunners. The heroes were following confused orders from higher military authority as they rode into this 'valley of Death'. Note the poet's words that 'Someone had blundered'....

THE CHARGE OF THE LIGHT BRIGADE

Half a league, half a league,
Half a league onward,
All in the valley of Death
    Rode the six hundred.
'Forward the Light Brigade!
Charge for the guns!' he said:
Into the valley of death
    Rode the six hundred.

'Forward the Light Brigade!'
Was there a man dismayed?
Not though the soldier knew
    Someone had blundered:
Theirs not to make reply,
Theirs not to reason why,
Theirs but to do and die:
Into the valley of Death
    Rode the six hundred.

Cannon to right of them,
Cannon to left of them,
Cannon in front of them
  Volleyed and thundered;
Stormed at with shot and shell,
Boldly they rode and well,
Into the jaws of Death,
Into the mouth of Hell
  Rode the six hundred.

Flashed all their sabres bare,
Flashed as they turned in air,
Sabring the gunners there,
Charging an army, while
  All the world wondered:
Plunged in the battery-smoke
Right through the line they broke;
Cossack and Russian
Reeled from the sabre-stroke
  Shattered and sundered.
Then they rode back, but not,
  Not the six hundred.

Cannon to right of them,
Cannon to left of them,
Cannon behind them
  Volleyed and thundered;
Stormed at with shot and shell,
While horse and hero fell,
They that had fought so well
Came through the jaws of Death,
Back from the mouth of Hell,
All that was left of them,
  Left of six hundred.

When can their glory fade?
O the wild charge they made!
  All the world wondered.
Honour the charge they made!
Honour the Light Brigade,
  Noble six hundred!

ALFRED, LORD TENNYSON

The Charge of the Light Brigade — Points to consider

(1) What were the two orders given to the six hundred as they rode into the valley of Death?

(2) 'Theirs not to make reply, / Theirs not to reason why, / Theirs but to do and die . . . .' Explain these famous lines in your own words.

(3) What is the third stanza describing?

(4) How did the cavalrymen attack the gunners?

(5) What do you think the poet means by 'All the world wondered'?

(6) 'Then they rode back, but not, / Not the six hundred.' Why not the six hundred?

(7) What do you think 'the jaws of Death' and 'the mouth of Hell' mean?

(8) What is the poet's message to the reader in the last stanza?

The beginning of World War II saw British armies that had been sent to France and Belgium trying vainly to oppose the German army as it swept victoriously across Europe and into France. The British were forced back to the coast where, surrounded on land and with their back to the sea, they made a stand at the French town of Dunkirk. Fleets of small ships and boats — even sailing-vessels — hastily set out from England to save the British troops from annihilation. In spite of fierce German bombing and shelling, most of the soldiers were rescued from the beaches and returned to England.

DUNKIRK, 1940

The little ships, the little ships
   Rushed out across the sea
To save the luckless armies
   From death and slavery.

From Tyne and Thames and Tamar,
   From the Severn and the Clyde,
The little ships, the little ships
   Went out in all their pride.

And home they brought their warriors,
   Weary and ragged and worn,
Back to the hills and shires
   And the towns where they were born.

Three hundred thousand warriors,
   From Hell to Home they came,
In the little ships, the little ships
   Of everlasting fame.

IDRIS DAVIES

Dunkirk, 1940 — What did you notice?

Did you notice that the poem is clearly divided into four stanzas, and that each stanza deals with a distinct thought or action? In a few words of your own, explain what each stanza is particularly concerned with.

The Brownshirts were the dedicated and fanatical followers of Hitler in pre–World War II Nazi Germany. In 'Song of a German Mother', the mother laments ever having encouraged her son to be a follower of *Der Führer* ('The Leader' — i.e. Hitler). Although this poem appears to concern only a mother and her son, it actually suggests the way in which a whole nation — the German nation — was led to destruction.

SONG OF A GERMAN MOTHER

My son, your shiny boots and
Brown shirt were a present from me:
If I'd known then what I know now
I'd have hanged myself from a tree.

My son, when I saw your hand raised
In the Hitler salute that first day
I didn't know those who saluted
Would see their hand wither away.

My son, I can hear your voice speaking:
Of a race of heroes it tells.
I didn't know, guess or see that
You worked in their torture cells.

My son, when I saw you marching
In Hitler's victorious train
I didn't know he who marched off then
Would never come back again.

My son, you told me our country
Was about to come into its own.
I didn't know all it would come to
Was ashes and bloodstained stone.

I saw you wearing your brown shirt.
I should have protested aloud
For I did not know what I now know:
It was your burial shroud.

BERTOLT BRECHT

Song of a German Mother — The promise and the horror

In each of the first five stanzas of the poem, the first and second lines deal with the glorious early days of the Nazi regime and the promise they seemed to hold. But the third and fourth lines of each stanza switch the reader to the horror of the result of Hitler's coming to power. Complete the following, stating the terrible result in each case.

(1)   The German mother had heard her son speaking of a race of heroes, not knowing or guessing that her son ....

(2)   She had watched her son marching in victory behind Hitler, not knowing that ....

(3)   She had been told by her son that Germany was about to come into its own, but she did not know that all it would come to would be ....

(4)   She had seen her son wearing his brown shirt, but she did not know that it was to become his ....

(5)   The mother had seen her son raise his hand in the Hitler salute, little knowing that those who saluted would ....

'Returned Soldier' is divided into two sections. The first describes the soldier's going to war, and the second his return. In the first section the soldier makes a promise to himself. In the second section we learn that the promise has been kept, but the cost has been high and the soldier's injuries terrible. Yet Barry, the returned soldier, has survived — and the poet realizes just what it was that gave Barry the will to live.

RETURNED SOLDIER

I put him on the train in Albury
The night he went to take his boat, and he,
Swinging aboard, called gaily, 'Don't forget,
I'll dodge them all and be a farmer yet,
And raise, for every bullet that goes by,
A stalk of wheat, red-gold and shoulder high,
Three hundred acres, lad!' And then the train
Was gone. The night was loud with frogs again.

And five years later, one November day,
I walked with Barry down the stooks of hay
Light yellow in the sun, and on them fluttered
Rosellas red as apples. Barry muttered
Half shyly as we faced the level wheat:
'One good foot left of what was once two feet,
One lung just fair, and one unclouded eye;
But all those years I heard them whining by
And in the mud I chuckled to remember
How wheat turns copper and gold in late November.'
He smiled, and then I knew what charm had brought
Him safely past 'the world's great snare', uncaught.

ERNEST G. MOLL

Returned Soldier — A powerful harvest

(1) What does the soldier mean by 'I'll dodge them all and be a farmer yet'?

(2) What words bring out the beauty of the wheat?

(3) How do you know that Barry was injured during the war?

(4) What kept him alive?

(5) What do you think is meant by 'the world's great snare'?

(6) What do you think is the poet's message to the reader?

Although a soldier must sometimes face the dangers and horrors of fighting in battle, there are also times when he must cope with the boredom and tedium of standing guard. In the following poem, a Roman soldier does guard duty on the battlements of a Roman wall.

In about AD 122 and the years following, the Emperor Hadrian had a great wall built across the north of what is now England to keep at bay the Picts and Scots, who were continuously attacking Roman Britain from the north. However, in this poem we forget about Hadrian (who was, after all, living it up in luxury down in Rome) and we focus on the hardships of an ordinary soldier standing guard on the wall. He is missing his girl in Tungria, a place in southern Italy where the sun is no doubt shining. Thoughts of his girl lead on to thoughts of others who might be hanging around her. Finally, the soldier spares a thought for the future.

ROMAN WALL BLUES

Over the heather the wet wind blows,
I've lice in my tunic and a cold in my nose.

The rain comes pattering out of the sky,
I'm a Wall soldier, I don't know why.

The mist creeps over the hard grey stone,
My girl's in Tungria; I sleep alone.

Aulus goes hanging around her place,
I don't like his manners, I don't like his face.

Piso's a Christian, he worships a fish;
There'd be no kissing if he had his wish.

She gave me a ring but I diced it away;
I want my girl and I want my pay.

When I'm a veteran with only one eye
I shall do nothing but look at the sky.

W. H. AUDEN

Roman Wall Blues — Suffering with the soldier

(1)   What things are irritating the soldier in the opening lines of the poem?

(2) Explain why 'pattering' is a good word to use for the sound of the falling rain.

(3) 'The mist creeps' suggests something that a person might do. What figure of speech is being used here?

(4) What does the soldier not like about Aulus?

(5) 'I shall do nothing but look at the sky.' Why does the soldier say that this is all he will do once he becomes a veteran?

'Revelation' — the word means 'a revealing or disclosing; a striking disclosure of something not previously realized'. The revelation in the poem that follows concerns towns on opposite sides during a war. Such towns, although on opposite sides, can be thought of as identical — in their suffering and in the ruin that war brings to them.

REVELATION

Machines of death from east to west
Drone through the darkened sky:
Machines of death from west to east
Through the same darkness fly.

They pass; and on the foredoomed towns
Loosen their slaughtering load:
They see no faces in the stones:
They hear no cries of blood.

They leave a ruin; and they meet
A ruin on return:
The mourners in the alien street
At their own doorways mourn.

WILLIAM SOUTAR

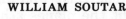

Revelation — What does the poem reveal?

(1) What are the machines of death?

(2) Why do they fly from different directions?

(3) What do you think 'foredoomed' means?

(4) What is 'their slaughtering load'?

(5) What are the 'faces in the stones'?

(6)   What are the 'cries of blood'?

(7)   In the third and fourth lines of the second stanza, who are 'They'?

(8)   'They leave a ruin; and they meet / A ruin on return . . . .' What are the two ruins?

(9)   Explain the last two lines of the poem.

(10) What is the poet's message in 'Revelation'?

Night bombers on a landing-ground must have been a familiar sight during World War II, and in this poem the sense of sight is very important. As you read, notice that the poet takes the silhouettes of the bombers against the sunrise, focuses on parts of the silhouettes (such as the wings) and conveys a strong sense of the job these parts perform in keeping the bombers airborne. Finally the poet looks at the bombers as whole shapes once again, and seems to feel them come alive. . . .

NIGHT BOMBERS ON A LANDING-GROUND

Darkly,
The great shapes lean against the sunrise.
The blades,
That all night long had bored into the wind;
The wings,
That rode the solid unseen aerial wave;
The frames,
That quivered with the stress and strain
Of motors locked in conflict with the night
Were silent, earthbound,
And at rest.
Black wheels anchored the sky-shapes to the soil,
Linking the sleeping spirits to the clod
And, as the East was kindled, as the sun appeared,
I thought the planes stirred softly,
Like berthed ships, that feel the tides change
In some sheltered harbour-place.

REGINALD GRIFFITHS

Night Bombers — Some effective images

(1)   What word tells us how the propellers bit into the wind?

(2)   Where was the wave the wings rode on?

(3) What other part of the plane caused the plane's airframes to quiver?

(4) In your own words explain the lines, 'Black wheels anchored the sky-shapes to the soil, / Linking the sleeping spirits to the clod'.

(5) 'And, as the East was kindled ....' The verb 'kindle' means 'set on fire, ignite'. Why do you think it is an appropriate word to use here?

(6) What did the planes seem to do as the sun appeared?

(7) To what are the planes compared in the last section of the poem?

(8) What does the poet suggest about the landing-ground where the bombers were standing?

Here is a little poem concerning war — its ultimate futility, and the sheer waste of human life. Before reading this poem you should know that the battles of Austerlitz and Waterloo involved Napoleon: the first was a great victory by him over the Austrians, while the second was his great defeat at the hands of the Duke of Wellington. Gettysburg was a battle of the American Civil War; Ypres and Verdun were terrible battles of World War I.

One thing common to many battlefields is the grass that soon covers over and smooths away all trace of the carnage. In the poem, notice that it is the grass itself which is speaking to us as it goes about its work. Also, notice how well the lesson of futility is brought home by the picture of passengers (perhaps on a train) travelling over the site of some famous battle, the scene of some horrible massacre, and asking the conductor 'What place is this? Where are we now?'

GRASS

Pile the bodies high at Austerlitz and Waterloo.
Shovel them under and let me work —
    I am the grass; I cover all.

And pile them high at Gettysburg
And pile them high at Ypres and Verdun.
Shovel them under and let me work.
Two years, ten years, and passengers ask the conductor:
    What place is this?
    Where are we now?

I am the grass.
Let me work.

CARL SANDBURG

22. Looking at Love

Love between two people can change with the passing of the years: it can become another casualty of time, or it can deepen and strengthen. 'When I'm Sixty-Four' takes a whimsical, cautious, but perhaps hopeful glance into the future.

WHEN I'M SIXTY-FOUR

When I get older losing my hair,
Many years from now,
Will you still be sending me a Valentine,
Birthday greetings bottle of wine?
If I'd been out till quarter to three
Would you lock the door?
Will you still need me, will you still feed me,
When I'm sixty-four?

You'll be older too,
And if you say the word,
I could stay with you.

I could be handy, mending a fuse
When your lights have gone;
You can knit a sweater by the fireside,
Sunday morning go for a ride;
Doing the garden, digging the weeds,
Who could ask for more?
Will you still need me, will you still feed me,
When I'm sixty-four?

Every summer we can rent a cottage
In the Isle of Wight, if it's not too dear;
We shall scrimp and save;
Grandchildren on your knee,
Vera, Chuck and Dave.

Send me a postcard, drop me a line,
Stating point of view;
Indicate precisely what you mean to say
Yours sincerely, wasting away.
Give me your answer, fill in a form,
Mine for evermore;
Will you still need me, will you still feed me,
When I'm sixty-four?

JOHN LENNON and PAUL McCARTNEY
(Recorded by The Beatles)

The ever-recurring story of Boy Meets Girl takes off in a new, powerful,
motorized form in the next poem.

COME LIVE WITH ME AND BE MY GIRL

If you'll give me a kiss and be my girl
Jump on my bike, we'll do a ton.
We'll explode from the city in a cloud of dust
And roar due west to the setting sun.

We'll bounce the days all over the beach
Pop them like seaweed and scatter ourselves
Careless as kids with candy floss
Into all the shapes of all the shells.

We'll go as giddy as merry-go-rounds,
Bump with a crash like dodgem cars,
Float in a basket of coloured balloons
Or jump in a rocket and whizz for Mars.

If you love to be blown by a roar of wind,
If you love to twist and spin and twirl,
If you love to crash on the shore like waves,
Then give me a kiss and be my girl.

I love to be blown by a roar of wind,
But I love to watch the sea asleep,
And breathe in salt and fresh-caught shrimps
As we wind our way through snoring streets.

I'll jive in a cellar till the band drops dead
But I want you to sing on your own guitar
For no one but me and a moonlight oak
Then dive in the silent lake for a star.

I love to twist the night away
But I love to hold you dark and still.
I love your kick that drives us miles
But I love the view from the top of the hill.

But if you give me the crashing waves
And sing me the blues of the sea as well,
Then, whether there's candyfloss or not,
I'll give you a kiss and be your girl.

                                    LEO AYLEN

Come Live with Me — A thought-provoking dialogue

(1)   The first stanza deals with the boy and girl taking off on the bike. What words and phrases contribute to the idea of power and speed?

(2)   How is the feeling of freedom expressed in the third stanza?

(3)   Who begins to speak in the fifth stanza?

(4)   Just about all the human senses are evoked in the fifth stanza? Give a sense-by-sense account.

(5)   How do the things the girl prefers to do differ in pace and spirit from those the boy finds attractive?

A *nocturne* is a dreamy or pensive piece of music, but the word also suggests something that takes place *at night*. The nocturne in this poem is certainly a piece of music, but it is emanating from the corner phonebox and is causing a person in a nearby room to imagine, rather dreamily, the purpose of the music. As you read through the poem notice the visions that the music produces in the mind of the listener. What *kind* of music is it? What change has developed in the listener by the end of the poem?

THE NOCTURNE IN THE CORNER PHONEBOX

Someone is playing a trombone
in the telephone box outside my room.
It's 1 a.m.
and he's removed the globe.
He's playing a melancholy cadenza
probably over the STD
to his girl in Sydney.

I can imagine . . .
she's curled to the telephone
listening to that impossible music
a smile curving her face.
I wonder if he has enough change
for all those extensions.
Could he reverse the charge?

Somebody called Hugh Adamson
blares out a nocturne in a phonebox.
His father's old and dying,
his mother's dead, his girl's away,
he's very sad, his nocturne's very sad,
his trombone blares and flares and says
'He's very sad, yair yair, he's very sad.'

Maybe he's only playing to a friend
in East St Kilda.
Maybe he hasn't any change.
Someone is playing a trombone — impossible —
in the phonebox with the door shut.
I've no idea who he is. I'm waiting
for my phone to ring. I like this music.

ANDREW TAYLOR

The splendid girls that drive by in fast cars are not for the writer of the next poem. Let him tell you why....

SPLENDID GIRLS

Those splendid girls at the wheels of powerful cars,
Sheer mechanism setting off slender charms.
I glimpse daredevil smiles as they whip past.

What are they all eager for, driving so fast
That I see them only momentarily? They are
Wholly desirable for half a heart-beat.

They have such style, such red nails! They are so neat!
But though they appear to drive at a dangerous speed
They do not do anything at random, that's for sure.

So keep your shirt on, they are spoken for.
They are as bright and lively as advertisements
For cigarettes or petrol or soap.

But there is no danger, and there is no hope.
Those reckless smiles have been carefully painted.
They are that sort of doll.

Everything, but everything, is under control.

JOHN NORMANTON

Splendid Girls — Reacting to the poem

(1) As we read through the opening stanza of the poem, we find the poet drawing a parallel between the girls and the cars they drive by the use of expressions that evoke, on the one hand, beauty (e.g. 'splendid girls') and, on the other hand, power (e.g. 'powerful cars'). Write down another expression in the first stanza which maintains this parallel.

(2) Why is the second stanza devoted to merely fleeting impressions and fleeting feelings?

(3) What does the man actually notice about the girls as they drive by in their cars?

(4) What point is the man really making when he compares the splendid girls to advertisements?

(5) How is the girls' deceptive appearance, which is brought out in the fourth stanza, developed in the fifth stanza?

(6) What firm opinion does the poet hold about their real motives?

(7) What kind of truth do you think this poem is showing us?

In this curious poem, the poet's loved one is described as 'Electric in her ways'. But you won't find out the shocking truth until the end of the poem.

ELECTRIC LOVE

My love is like a dynamo
With woven wire for hair,
And when she brushes it at night
The sparks run crackling there.

Oh she is the magnetic field
In which I pass my days,
And she will always be to me
Electric in her ways.

No insulated force is she;
Galvanic rather, seeing
Hers is the current keeping bright
My filament of being.

Oh yes, my love's a dynamo
Who charges all the air;
My love is an Electrolux
Who sings upon the stair.

DENIS GLOVER

A great deal of effort was needed to win the free-selector's daughter, but her kiss was worth it.

THE FREE-SELECTOR'S DAUGHTER

I met her on the Lachlan-side —
    A darling girl I thought her,
And ere I left I swore I'd win
    The free-selector's daughter.

I milked her father's cows a month,
    I brought the wood and water,
I mended all the broken fence,
    Before I won the daughter.

I listened to her father's yarns,
    I did just what I 'oughter',
And what *you'll* have to do to win
    A free-selector's daughter.

I broke my pipe and burnt my twist,
    And washed my mouth with water;
I had a shave before I kissed
    The free-selector's daughter.

Then, rising in the frosty morn,
    I brought the cows for Mary,
And when I'd milked a bucketful
    I took it to the dairy.

I poured the milk into the dish
    While Mary held the strainer,
I summoned heart to speak my wish,
    And oh! her blush grew plainer.

I told her I must leave the place,
    I said that I would miss her;
At first she turned away her face,
    And then she let me kiss her.

I put the bucket on the ground,
    And in my arms I caught her:
I'd give the world to hold again
    That free-selector's daughter!

HENRY LAWSON

23. People and Machines

In the following sonnet, Louis Untermeyer issues us with a warning: that the machine is quietly taking over.

PORTRAIT OF A MACHINE

What nudity as beautiful as this
Obedient monster purring at its toil;
Those naked iron muscles dripping oil,
And the sure-fingered rods that never miss?
This long and shining flank of metal is
Magic that greasy labour cannot spoil;
While this vast engine that could rend the soil
Conceals its fury with a gentle hiss.

It does not vent its loathing, it does not turn
Upon its makers with destroying hate.
It bears a deeper malice; lives to earn
Its master's bread and laughs to see this great
Lord of the earth, who rules but cannot learn,
Become the slave of what his slaves create.

LOUIS UNTERMEYER

Portrait of a Machine — Careful consideration

(1) What words in the first five lines suggest that the machine is living?
(2) Name two qualities of the machine which the poet seems to praise in the first eight lines.
(3) What words suggest that the machine is powerful?
(4) Look carefully at the last word of each of the first eight lines in turn. Say the words to yourself: *this ... toil ... oil ... miss ... is ... spoil ... soil ... hiss.* What does the sound of these words remind you of?
(5) What is the machine's attitude to its master?

(6) 'Lord of the earth, who rules but cannot learn, / Become the slave of what his slaves create.' Explain what these lines mean.

(7) A portrait usually depicts a *person*. Why do you think the poet has used the word 'portrait' rather than 'picture' or 'description'?

(8) What is the poet's message to his readers in this poem?

People who enjoy their work should be thankful. Here is a description of a job that numbs the brain.

THE RELEASE

All day he shoves the pasteboard in
The slick machine that turns out boxes,
A box a minute; and its din
Is all his music, as he stands
And feeds it; while his jaded brain
Moves only out and in again
With the slick motion of his hands,
Monotonously making boxes,
A box a minute — all his thoughts
A slick succession of empty boxes.

But, when night comes, and he is free
To play his fiddle, with the music
His whole soul moves to melody;
No more recalling day's dumb round,
His reckless spirit sweeps and whirls
On surging waves and dizzy swirls
And eddies of enchanted sound;
And in a flame-winged flight of music
Above the roofs and chimneys soars
To ride the starry tides of music.

w. w. GIBSON

The Release — Working on the poem

(1) Why is the machine-operator's brain so 'jaded' (worn out)?

(2) What words suggest that the machine-operator does his job well?

(3) What contrast is there between night and day for the machine-operator?

(4) Explain the meaning of 'day's dumb round'.

(5) What do the words 'eddies of enchanted sound' mean? What other words carry on this idea?

(6) 'His reckless spirit sweeps and whirls . . . .' What has happened to the machine-operator?

(7) Why is the poem called 'The Release'?

Considering the Issues

(1) Do you think young people would be better off accepting the dole than doing the kind of work described in 'The Release'?

(2) Do you think working hours should be reduced so as to provide more time for leisure?

Who but a poet would have thought of comparing a garbage truck to a huge hunched animal?

GARBAGE TRUCK

The garbage disposal truck
Like a huge hunched animal
That sucks in garbage in the place
Where other animals evacuate it
Whines, as the cylinder in the rear
Threshes up the trash and garbage,
Where two men in rubber suits
(It must be raining outside)
Heap it in. The groaning motor
Rises in a whine as it grinds in
The garbage, and between-times
Groans. It whines and groans again.
All about it as it moves down
5th Street is the clatter of trashcans,
The crashes of them as the sanitary engineers
Bounce them on the sidewalk.
If it is raining outside
You can only tell by looking
In puddles, under the lifted streetlamps.

It would be the spring rain.

GALWAY KINNELL

Sometimes a car possesses all the traits of a wild animal. Read 'Jaguar' and see whether you agree.

JAGUAR

Sleek-bodied,
With gleaming flanks.
Nature's latest model.
Caught in the rays of the afternoon's dying sun
For a brief moment,
The light shining and rippling down the long smooth side.
There she stands,
Purring gently,
Engine ticking over.

Then,
Deftly, gracefully,
She moves into first gear;
Slides forward,
Gathers speed;
Until with throttle open
She utters her full-throated roar,
And unleashed
Leaps across the intersection —
Steel-muscled acrobat
Arching through the dark.

But suddenly the light
Thins sharply.
She starts to brake,
Veers swiftly to the left,
Decelerates rapidly,
But cannot pause
Before the last great mounting spring . . .
And now, as she strikes,
Her front rears up
Agonisingly . . .

A crunch of severed muscle,
Twisted sinew and seared flesh,
A splendid face ripped out of recognition.

And I wonder, with my dying breath,
That this superb machine was built
For death.

D. J. BRINDLEY

Jaguar — A poetry card

Copy the poetry card into your books and then fill in the details for the poem 'Jaguar'.

Poem's title: ....

Poet's name: ....

Subject matter (what the poem is about): ....
....
....
....

Message (the main idea the poet is trying to communicate to the reader):...
....

Word choice (some of the words that convey the idea of beauty, movement, destruction): ....
....
....
....

Your reaction (what aspects of the poem you like and/or dislike):
....
....
....
....

W. H. Davies, a famous writer, spent most of his life as a tramp. But tragedy struck when he was jumping a train in America. The poet D. J. Brindley tells the story.

FREE RIDE

Jumping trains
Used to be great fun
In the old days.
You leapt
At the shining mass of steel,
As with piston thrusts
And giant wheels turning
She powered her prodigious way
Out of the station,
Or slowed momentarily
Round a perilous bend.

You would run alongside
As she gathered glittering speed,
And then, at the footplate, spring —
And clutch —
And cling —
Like a panther holding to its prey.

But one day,
Of a tramp's long indolent summer,
There was hardly room for two
As we sped from a crouching hollow,
And he jumped with a breathless dash,
And I to follow.

I only remember the flash
And a scream of spinning steel,
As a foot swung loose and entangled
In the cutting metal wheel,
And they say a whistle of pain
Rose high from the shattered heel.

They later severed my leg
From the knee-cap down:
I paid the price of a limb
For a ride to town.

And now?

When I travel alone,
Treading the long world on a stump,
I sometimes listen at night
For the sudden jolting bump
And the unsympathetic whine
Of the train as it twists its way
On the forlorn tracks of time
To an eternity of day.

D. J. BRINDLEY

Free Ride — Some questions

(1) 'Jumping trains / Used to be great fun / In the old days.' Why did it cease to be fun?

(2) What words in the poem show us the power and the might of the train?

(3) When, according to the poet, are the best times to leap onto a moving train?

(4) 'Like a panther holding to its prey.' Why is this simile appropriate?

(5) How did the accident occur?

(6) 'And a scream of spinning steel . . . .' Point out the alliteration in this line and comment on its effect.

(7) Why do you think the poet called his poem 'Free Ride'? What penalty was paid for the ride?

(8) What clue in the last stanza indicates that Davies continued to lead the life of a tramp?

Being a wagondriver can present difficulties that most people would find unbearable.

SONG OF THE WAGONDRIVER

My first love was the ten-ton truck
They gave me when I started,
And though she played the bitch with me
I grieved when we were parted.

Since then I've had a dozen more,
The wound was quick to heal,
And now it's easier to say
I'm married to my wheel.

I've trucked it north, I've trucked it south,
On wagons good and bad,
But none was ever really like
The first I ever had.

The life is hard, the hours are long,
Sometimes I cease to feel,
But I go on, for it seems to me
I'm married to my wheel.

Often I think of my home and kids,
Out on the road at night,
And think of taking a local job
Provided the money's right.

Two nights a week I see my wife,
And eat a decent meal,
But otherwise, for all my life,
I'm married to my wheel.

                                        B. S. JOHNSON

Song of the Wagondriver — A marriage of necessity

(1) What does the wagondriver mean by 'she played the bitch with me'?

(2) What evidence can you find to show that the driver was very fond of the truck he started with?

(3) How do you know that the wagondriver has been driving trucks for
a long time?

(4) 'The life is hard,' he tells us. What makes his life so hard?

(5) 'I'm married to my wheel.' Comment on the driver's use of the word
'married'.

(6) What is B. S. Johnson's message to the reader in 'Song of the
Wagondriver'?

Here is a lively and graphic description of trains being washed and cleaned
so that they can face the public once again.

SHUNTING

These trucks and coaches, only yesterday,
Rolled through home counties, mile on metal mile,
Some with smooth speed, their open eyes of glass
Pupilled with passengers, while others went
Jolting along with homely jobs to do
From town to town. Now all alike assemble
Like branded sheep in this impartial yard;
Where they are rounded up with clank and puff,
And driven with efficient fuss of steam.
The whistling engine moves an inch, and sends
Concussions jumping down the coupled line;
Men wash the coaches clean with dripping mops,
Or step with peril among treacherous rails
To shift the levers which will organise,
Sort, and divide these trains that will be seen
Going on peaceful errands through green shires
With splendid salutations of white smoke.

BASIL DOWLING

Shunting — Some things to notice

(1) There are three time-periods in 'Shunting' — past, present and future.
Where were the trucks and carriages yesterday? What is happening
to them now? What will they be doing tomorrow?

(2)   The phrase 'mile on metal mile' is an example of alliteration. What does the repetition of the consonant 'm' suggest? What other examples of alliteration can you find in the poem?

(3)   'Like branded sheep' is a simile. What words in the next two lines carry on this comparison?

(4)   What words in the poem echo the actual sounds made by the trains?

(5)   What are the carriages' 'open eyes of glass'?

(6)   What picture of the carriage windows do the words 'Pupilled with passengers' give you?

(7)   'Concussions jumping down the coupled line . . . .' What is happening?

CAR SALESMAN

Framed in his showroom, tinted and furbished well —
A slide projected on the plastic wall —
The salesman hangs in wait to sell;

Till the buyer's tread, like a button touched or bell rung,
Signalling animation, jerks him to life,
Unwinds the message taped across his tongue;

Minces and mimics, hides a youth's pink pride,
And, lubricated with hypocrisy,
Insists on taking madame for a ride.

Row on row the new cars snarl and grin
Behind him — crouched, obsequious, and yet
With quiet irony content to hem him in.

Their pulsing synthesis of pipes and pistons, thrust and curled
In steel, remain no more insensitive than he,
Poor nerveless puppet of the brave new world;

Effete and unaware, he helps traduce
His heart; sells car and birthright glibly. On the wall
A graph like a whiplash bends him to its use.

He and his product from the same production line,
Ducoed with gloss, pretension and conceit,
Both advertise the altars of our time.

COLIN THIELE

Car Salesman — Some thoughts to consider

(1)   The car salesman is referred to as a 'puppet'. Write down two other phrases that suggest the salesman is being manipulated.

(2)   What does 'lubricated with hypocrisy' mean? Suggest a reason for the poet's use of 'lubricated'.

(3)   What is the poet's attitude to the car salesman?

(4)   What do you think 'obsequious' means?

(5)   Explain what 'the altars of our time' are?

(6)   What does the poet mean by 'He and his product from the same production line'?

(7)   What is the meaning of 'he helps traduce / His heart'?

(8)   Find a word in the poem which has a meaning similar to 'pretension'.

(9)   Explain why the simile 'like a whiplash' is effective.

(10) Did the poem appeal to you? Explain why or why not?

24. Down to the Seas

The Jamaican fisherman may be poor in his present possessions, but in his 'proud descent' he is a chief and a king. To the poet, the physical appearance of the fisherman proclaims his dignity and recalls the rich, dark land from which his ancestors came.

JAMAICAN FISHERMAN

Across the sand I saw a black man stride
To fetch his fishing gear and broken things,
And silently that splendid body cried
Its proud descent from ancient chiefs and kings.
Across the sand I saw him naked stride;
Sang his black body in the sun's white light
The velvet coolness of dark forests wide,
The blackness of the jungle's starless night.
He stood beside the old canoe which lay
Upon the beach; swept up within his arms
The broken nets and careless lounged away
Towards his wretched hut ...
Nor knew how fiercely spoke his body then
Of ancient wealth and savage regal men.

P. M. SHERLOCK

Jamaican Fisherman — Fishing for the clues
(1) What clues tell you that the fisherman is now living in poverty?
(2) What clues indicate that the fisherman's ancestors were of royal blood?
(3) What clues tell you that the fisherman has an impressive physique?

Plunge in — and the strange and magical world of the seabed is revealed. As you read this poem, you will come across some rich and unusual expressions and descriptions, such as 'the tune of the tide' and 'in seaweed furled'. Hover over these and others for a moment, and allow them to seep into your imagination. Towards the end of the poem comes the implied contrast between the wonders of the deep and the humdrum life ashore, which the diver is sorry to see looming up all too soon. . . .

THE DIVER

I put on my aqua-lung and plunge,
Exploring, like a ship with a glass keel,
The secrets of the deep. Along my lazy road
On and on I steal* —
Over waving bushes which at a touch explode
Into shrimps, then closing rock to the tune of the tide;
Over crabs that vanish in puffs of sand.
Look, a string of pearls bubbling at my side
Breaks in my hand —
Those pearls were my breath. . . . Does that hollow hide
Some old Armada wreck in seaweed furled,
Crusted with barnacles, her cannon rusted,
The great *San Philip*? What bullion in her hold?
Pieces of eight, silver crowns, and bars of solid gold?

I shall never know. Too soon the clasping cold
Fastens on flesh and limb
And pulls me to the surface. Shivering, back I swim
To the beach, the noisy crowds, the ordinary world.

IAN SERRAILLIER

* *steal*: move quietly and cautiously

The Diver — Into the poem

(1) What attitude or feeling do you think the diver wants to convey to us in the phrase 'my lazy road'?

(2) What happens to the 'waving bushes' when the diver touches them?

(3) In your own words explain 'rock to the tune of the tide'. What figure of speech is being used here?

(4) What is the 'string of pearls' mentioned by the poet?

(5)   Why is 'furled' a good word to choose to describe the way the sea-weed has grown over the wreck?

(6)   What do you see in your mind's eye when you read 'Crusted with barnacles'?

(7)   Why is 'clasping' a good word to use for cold?

(8)   What forces the diver to return to the surface?

Through every line of the famous poem below runs a stirring rhythm that comes across best if you read the poem aloud. Is it the rhythm of the waves sweeping by? or of a ship flying before the breeze? You decide. Whatever it represents, the rhythm is there running through the poem — in the very way the poet claims that the sea fever is running through his veins.

Before you begin reading, note the meanings of the following words you'll come across in the poem: *spume* is sea foam, froth or scum; *vagrant* means 'wandering, homeless'; *whetted* means 'sharpened by rubbing on a whetstone' (a stone for sharpening edged tools); *trick* is a seafaring term referring to a turn or spell at the wheel or helm.

SEA FEVER

I must go down to the seas again, to the lonely sea and the sky,
And all I ask is a tall ship and a star to steer her by,
And the wheel's kick and the wind's song and the white sail's
    shaking,
And a grey mist on the sea's face, and a grey dawn breaking.

I must go down to the seas again, for the call of the running tide
Is a wild call and a clear call that may not be denied;
And all I ask is a windy day with the white clouds flying,
And the flung spray and the blown spume, and the sea-gulls crying.

I must go down to the seas again, to the vagrant gypsy life,
To the gull's way and the whale's way where the wind's like a whet-
    ted knife;
And all I ask is a merry yarn from a laughing fellow-rover,
And quiet sleep and a sweet dream when the long trick's over.

JOHN MASEFIELD

Sea Fever — Listening to the poem

(1) The poet keeps repeating 'I must go down to the seas again'. What is it about the sea which makes him say this?

(2) The terms 'the sea's face' and 'the wind's song' are examples of personification. Explain in what way the sea and the wind have become human.

(3) Why is the life of a sailor 'the vagrant gypsy life'?

(4) What quality of the wind is the poet emphasizing when he describes it as 'like a whetted knife'?

(5) Why is 'Sea Fever' a good title for Masefield's poem?

The next poem is about the miniature world of the sea-anemone; the poet tells of an encounter with the small creature. The anemone is clinging with its tendrils extended and these, to the poet, are like fingers. But when he takes the anemone in his hand, the 'fingers are withdrawn' and nothing the poet can do will make the creature 'flower again', or even remain. Instead it sinks down into the sea and is lost.

THE ANEMONE

Under this ledge of rock a brown
And soft anemone clings,
Spreading his fingers to the sea
Deliciously.
I kneel down on the sand,
And squeezing gently with my thumb
I loose his hold and take him in my hand.
But now how swift his fingers are withdrawn! —
His tendrils shrunk and gone!
I dabble him and water him in vain —
He will not flower again;
And though I press him firmly to his rock,
He will not stick again or cling,
But sinks disconsolately down,
And is lost, poor thing!

JOHN WALSH

The Anemone — Look but don't touch!

This poem is appealing because such a moment — of reaching out for beauty only to see it perish or vanish as a consequence — is something within the experience of every human being. Think of and describe such an occurrence, either from your own experience or from something you have heard about or read.

Swimming down at the pool after school? Most of us have been there and done it, along with many of the other things Pam Ayres delights in mentioning.

THE SWIMMING SONG

I like to swim
I'll meet you after school
It keeps us trim
I'll see you down the pool
It keeps us fit
Watch out we're on the prowl
We do our bit
Talcum powder and a towel
Both great and small
Watch us on the diving board
Life savers all
Duke of Edinburgh's Award
If we're around
We're demons in the drink
You won't get drowned
We never ever sink.

We swim like fish
Cod, kipper, cockle, carp
Here, there, gone, swish!
Oh play it on your harp
And diving too
In the deep dark dregs
Just me and you
We'll be laughing at the legs
Just name the stroke
Oh, the butterfly and crawl
And I'm your bloke
Will you give me back my ball?
I love to spring
Plunge plink plonk paddle
It makes me sing
Tra la diddle daddle.

We're in the shower
Shampoo soap scrub
For half an hour
Rub a dub a dub a dub
Do you know that
Dad gave me fifty pence
You aren't half fat
Ouch! Eek! No offence!
It's great to swim
Never any pain or ache
It keeps us slim
Would you like a piece of cake?
So after school
If you have an hour to spend
Come to the pool
We'll race you to the end.

PAM AYRES

A Kraken is a fabled sea-monster. In his poem 'The Kraken', Tennyson shares with us his vision of a great monster of the deep. The poem describes in general terms the location of the Kraken; it then tells us about his fearful habitat, the immense creatures that share it with him, and his eventual death. 'The Kraken' is a poem that works powerfully on the imagination. Can you explain why?

THE KRAKEN

Below the thunders of the upper deep;
Far far beneath in the abysmal sea,
His ancient, dreamless, uninvaded sleep
The Kraken sleepeth: faintest sunlights flee
About his shadowy sides: above him swell
Huge sponges of millennial growth and height;
And far away into the sickly light,
From many a wondrous grot and secret cell
Unnumber'd and enormous polypi
Winnow with giant fins the slumbering green.
There hath he lain for ages and will lie
Battening upon huge seaworms in his sleep,
Until the latter fire shall heat the deep;
Then once by men and angels to be seen,
In roaring he shall rise and on the surface die.

ALFRED, LORD TENNYSON

The Kraken — Questions in depth

(1) What would you say are 'the thunders of the upper deep'?

(2) In the second line of the poem, 'abysmal' means 'bottomless' or 'unfathomable'. Why do you think the poet has chosen such a word to describe where the Kraken lives?

(3) 'The Kraken sleepeth: faintest sunlights flee / About his shadowy sides . . . .' Describe in your own words what is conjured up in your imagination.

(4) If 'millennial' means 'of a thousand years', what do you understand by 'Huge sponges of millennial growth and height'?

25. Tombstone Poetry

EPITAPH FOR JOHN BUN

Here lies John Bun,
He was killed by a gun,
His name was not Bun, but Wood,
But Wood would not rhyme with gun, but Bun would.

Here lie G. Whilliken's friends, all five.
He took them along when he learned to drive.

Here lieth the mother of children seven,
Four on earth and three in Heaven —
The three in Heaven preferring rather
To die with Mother than live with Father.

LATHER AS YOU GO

Beneath this slab,
John Brown is stowed.
He watched the ads,
And not the road.

OGDEN NASH

MY EPITAPH

Here lie I, bereft of breath,
Because a cough
Carried me off;
Then a coffin
They carried me off in.

ON A TIRED HOUSEWIFE

Here lies a poor woman who was always tired,
She lived in a house where help wasn't hired:
Her last words on earth were: 'Dear friends, I am going
To where there's no cooking, or washing, or sewing,
For everything there is exact to my wishes,
For where they don't eat there's no washing of dishes.
I'll be where loud anthems will always be ringing,
But having no voice I'll be quit of the singing.
Don't mourn for me now, don't mourn for me never,
I am going to do nothing for ever and ever '

A CHILD OF SEVEN MONTHS

If I am so quickly done for
What on earth was I begun for?

Beneath this stone, a lump of clay,
Lies Uncle Peter Dan'el's
Who, early in the month of May,
Took off his winter flannels.

Under this sod
And under these trees
Lieth the bod-
y of Solomon Pease.
He's not in this hole,
But only his pod;
He shelled out his soul
And went up to his God.

ON A HASTY WOMAN

Here lies the body of Mary Chowder,
She burst while drinking a Seidlitz Powder;
She couldn't wait till it effervesced,
So now she's gone to eternal rest.

A HUSBAND'S DEATH

As I am now so you must be
Therefore prepare to follow me.

THE WIFE'S EPITAPH

To follow you I'm not content
How do I know which way you went?

Acknowledgements

The authors and publishers are grateful to the following for permission to reproduce copyright material.

Poems and poem extracts: Macmillan Limited for 'Swift Things Are Beautiful' by Elizabeth Coatsworth from *Away Goes Sally*, 'My Grandmother' by Elizabeth Jennings from *Collected Poems 1967* and 'The Release' by W. W. Gibson; Thomas Nelson Australia for 'Pleasant Sounds' by John Clare from *Poetry Workshop* by Russell and Chatfield, and 'Raindrop' by John Travers Moore; Methuen & Company Ltd for 'Smells' by Christopher Morley from *Chimney Smoke*, 'Boots' by Rudyard Kipling from *The Complete Barrack-Room Ballads of Rudyard Kipling* and 'Song of a German Mother' by Bertolt Brecht; Oxford University Press for 'First Dip' by John Walsh, 'First Frost' by Andrei Voznesensky, 'Elegy for Alfred Hubbard' by Tony Connor and 'Portrait of a Machine' by Louis Untermeyer; Anne Holman for 'Poems'; New Directions Publishing Corporation for 'This Is Just to Say' by Wiliam Carlos Williams; Lothian Publishing Company for 'The Shearer's Wife' by Louis Esson; Angus & Robertson Publishers for 'West of Alice' by W. E. Harney, 'Tangmalangaloo' by John O'Brien, 'Country Towns' by Kenneth Slessor, 'An Aboriginal Simile' by Mary Gilmore, 'Tree Poem' by W. Hart-Smith, 'Tea Talk' and 'The Band' by C. J. Dennis, 'Lady Feeding the Cats' by Douglas Stewart, 'Foxes among the Lambs', 'At the Pool' and 'Returned Soldier' by Ernest G. Moll, 'Trapped Dingo' and 'The Killer' by Judith Wright, 'William Street' by Kenneth Slessor, 'Our Father' by Ray Mathew, 'The Frog Pool' by James Devaney, 'Dead Swagman' by Nancy Cato, and 'The Crabs' by Brian Vrepont from *Beyond the Claw*; Retusa for 'Waltzing Matilda' and 'Old Man Platypus' by A. B. ('Banjo') Paterson; Society of Authors for 'Reynard the Fox' and 'Sea Fever' by John Masefield; British Broadcasting Corporation for 'Caterpillar' by Martin Thornton, 'In the Bath' by Stephen Hewitt and 'Muddy Boots' by Philip Paddon from *My World — Poems from Living Language* by Joan Griffiths; William Heinemann Limited for 'Fireworks', 'The Sea' and 'Mr Kartoffel' by James Reeves; Faber and Faber Limited for 'Folks' and 'My Mother' by Ted Hughes, 'Late Night Walk down Terry Street' by Douglas Dunn from *Terry Street*, extract from *Archy and Mehitabel* and 'book review' by Don Marquis, 'The Unknown Citizen' and 'Roman Wall Blues' by W. H. Auden, 'Jigsaws' by Louis MacNeice, and 'Dunkirk, 1940' by Idris Davies from *Tonypandy*; Pam Ayres for 'Where There's a Will' from *Some More of Me Poetry*, 'The Wasp He Is a Nasty One' from *Thoughts of a Late-night Knitter*, 'Please Will You Take Your Children Home Before I Do Them In', 'I'm the Dog Who Didn't Win a Prize' and 'The Swimming Song' from *The Ballad of Bill Spinks Bedstead*; Doubleday and Co. Inc. for 'My Papa's Waltz' by Theodore Roethke; Andre Deutsch Ltd for 'My Dad's Thumb', 'My Brother Is Making a Protest about Bread' and 'I've Had This Shirt' by Michael Rosen from *Mind Your Own Business*; Northern Songs Pty Ltd for 'She's Leaving Home' and 'When I'm Sixty-four' by John Lennon and Paul McCartney; Edward Arnold (Publishers) Ltd for 'Uncle' and 'Politeness' by Harry Graham and 'The Shark' by Lord Alfred Douglas; Penguin Books Ltd for 'The ABC', 'My Sister Laura', 'Today I Saw a Little Worm' and 'Hello Mr Python' by Spike Milligan from *Silly Verse for Kids* and 'Giraffes' by Mary Ann Hoberman from *The Raucous Ark*; William Jay Smith for 'The Toaster'; Holt Rinehart and Winston Ltd for 'Steam Shovel' by Charles Malam from *Upper Pasture*; Beatrice Janosco for 'The Garden Hose'; Etsuro Sakamoto for 'Subway'; Gerald Raftery for 'Apartment House'; *Education* (Journal of NSW Teachers' Federation) for 'Our New Teacher' by David Bateson; Harper & Row Ltd for 'Sick' by Shel Silverstein; R. C. Scriven for 'The Marrog'; Australian Consolidated Press for 'Woman of the Future' by Cathy Warry from *The Australian Women's Weekly*

241

(24/12/75); Rigby Publishers for 'Bird in the Classroom', 'Why Did They Knock Down the Trees, Daddy?' and 'Car Salesman' by Colin Thiele; Hope Leresche and Sayle for 'First Day at School' by Roger McGough; Val Kostic for 'Freedom of Speech'; Franklin Watts Ltd for 'How Sad' by William Cole; Macmillan Inc. for 'The Wind' by James Stephens from *Collected Poems* and 'Corner' by Ralph Pomeroy from *In the Financial District*; Putnam & Co. Ltd for 'Snow' by Dorothy Aldis from *Everything and Anything*; Burke Publishing Co. Ltd for 'My Friend Luigi' by John Smith from *The Early Bird and the Worm*; Alan Wells for 'The Housewife's Lament'; A. Elliott-Cannon for 'Fish and Chips'; Longman Cheshire Pty Limited for 'Drifters' by Bruce Dawe from *Sometimes Gladness*; Japan Publications Inc. for Japanese haiku on pp. 93-4; Random House Inc. for two haiku by Paul Goodman from *Hawkweed*; Joe Rosenblatt for 'Waiter! . . . There's an Alligator in My Coffee'; Hadley Records and Yeldah Music for 'The Redback on the Toilet Seat' by Slim Newton (R. E. Newton); Max Dunn for 'The Onomatopoeia River'; Gareth Owen for 'Ping-Pong'; Australian National University Press for 'Old Man Possum' by Geoffrey Lehmann; Columbia University Press for 'The Panther' by Rainer Maria Rilke; Allans Music Australia for 'Cats on the Roof' by Edward Harrington; Curtis Brown Group Limited and the Estate of Ogden Nash for 'The Rhinoceros', 'Song of the Open Road' and 'Lather As You Go' by Ogden Nash; E. B. White for 'Dog around the Block' from *The Fox of Peapack and Other Poems*; Gerald Duckworth and Co. Ltd for 'Tarantella' by Hilaire Belloc; Colin Bingham for 'Sad Song at Surfer's'; Victor Gollancz Ltd for 'Superman' and 'On the Inclusion of Miniature Dinosaurs in Breakfast Cereal Boxes' by John Updike; The New Yorker Magazine Inc. for 'Summer Song' by W. W. Watts; Marie Zbierski for 'Mosquito'; D. Sadler for 'Smile'; Andrew James for 'Sausage Poem'; Charles Scribner's Sons for 'Supermarket' by Felice Holman; Carol Elliot for 'Moustache'; The Hogarth Press Ltd and Mrs Elna Lucas for 'Beleaguered Cities' by F. L. Lucas from *Time and Money*; Essex Music Australia Pty Ltd for 'Little Boxes' by M. Reynolds; John Murray Publishers Ltd for 'Harvest Hymn' by John Betjeman; Longman Group Ltd for 'Coverings' by Stella Gibbons; Kath Walker for 'No More Boomerang'; Sheed and Ward Ltd for 'The Mason' by Robert Farren; William Blackwood and Sons Ltd for 'The Highwayman' by Alfred Noyes; The Hogarth Press Ltd and Mr C. Day Lewis for 'Flying to New Zealand' by Michael Thwaites; Melbourne University Press for 'Boxing On' by Evan Jones from *Understandings*; *Read Magazine*, Xerox Education Group, for 'Foul Shot' by Edwin A. Hoey; Liveright Publishing Corporation for 'Those Winter Sundays' by Robert Hayden from *New and Selected Poems*; University of Michigan Press for 'The Crabs' by Richard Lattimore; Reginald Griffiths Esq. for 'Night Bombers on a Landing-ground' by Reginald Griffiths; Jonathan Cape Ltd for 'Grass' by Carl Sandburg from *Cornhuskers*; Sidgwick and Jackson Ltd for 'Come Live with Me and Be My Girl' by Leo Aylen from *Sunflower*; University of Queensland Press for 'The Nocturne in the Corner Phonebox' by Andrew Taylor from *The Cool Change*; Denis Glover for 'Electric Love'; Houghton Mifflin Publishers for 'Garbage Truck' by Galway Kinnell from *What a Kingdom It Was*; D. J. Brindley for 'Jaguar' and 'Free Ride'; Constable and Co. Ltd for 'Song of the Wagondriver' by B. S. Johnson; The Caxton Printers Ltd for 'Shunting' by Basil Dowling; John Walsh for 'The Anemone'; Oxford University Press and Ian Serraillier for 'The Diver' by Ian Serraillier.

Comic strips: Murray Ball p. 111; John Fairfax and Sons Ltd p. 130; Alan Foley Pty Ltd p. 53; United Feature Syndicate p. 115.

Drawings: Randy Glusac.

Cover: Jan Schmoeger.

We would like to express our appreciation to our editor, Alex Skovron,
for all his guidance, help and creativity.

Index of Poems

Index of Poets